FINAL PROGRAMMATIC ENVIRONMENTAL IMPACT STATEMENT FOR SEAGRASS RESTORATION IN THE FLORIDA KEYS NATIONAL MARINE SANCTUARY

August 23, 2004

Prepared by:

National Oceanic and Atmospheric Administration
1305 East-West Highway
Silver Spring, Maryland 20910
(Contact: Harriet Sopher: 301-713-3125 ext. 109)

and

Florida Department of Environmental Protection
216 Ann Street
Key West, FL 33040
(Contact: Anne McCarthy: 305-292-0311)

TABLE OF CONTENTS

APPENDIX B. COMMENTS RECEIVED ON THE DRAFT PROGRAMMATIC ENVIRONMENTAL IMPACT STATEMENT FOR SEAGRASS RESTORATION AND RESPONSES TO COMMENTS..72

LIST OF ACRONYMS

ACOE	Army Corps of Engineers
CE	Categorical Exclusion
CZMA	Coastal Zone Management Act
DPEIS	Draft Programmatic Environmental Impact Statement
EA	Environmental Assessment
EFH	Essential Fish Habitat
EIS	Environmental Impact Statement
EPCRA	Emergency Planning and Community Right-to-Know Act
ERP	Environmental Resource Permit
ESA	Endangered Species Act
FDEP	Florida Department of Environmental Protection
FKNMS	Florida Keys National Marine Sanctuary
FKNMSPA	Florida Keys National Marine Sanctuary and Protection Act
FMRI	Florida Marine Research Institute
FONSI	Finding of No Significant Impact
FPEIS	Final Programmatic Environmental Impact Statement
HEA	Habitat Equivalency Analysis
MLLW	Mean Lower Low Water
MMS	Minerals Management Service
NAAQS	National Ambient Air Quality Standards
NAO	NOAA Administrative Order
NEPA	National Environmental Policy Act
NMSA	National Marine Sanctuary Act
NOAA	National Oceanic and Atmospheric Administration
NRDA	Natural Resource Damage Assessment
PEIS	Programmatic Environmental Impact Statement
POL	Petroleum, Oil, or Lubricant
PU	Planting Unit
PVC	Polyvinyl Chloride
ROI	Region of Influence
SHPO	State Historic Preservation Officer
SIP	State Implementation Plan
USC	United States Code
USDOC	United States Department of Commerce
USEPA	United States Environmental Protection Agency

CHAPTER 1. PURPOSE AND NEED FOR ACTION

1.1 PURPOSE

This Programmatic Environmental Impact Statement (PEIS) systematically evaluates the short and long-term environmental and socioeconomic effects related to the implementation of seagrass restoration and seagrass injury prevention projects in the Florida Keys National Marine Sanctuary (FKNMS). The Trustees for the FKNMS are the National Oceanic and Atmospheric Administration (NOAA) and the Board of Trustees of the Internal Improvement Trust Fund of the State of Florida ("State of Florida" or "State"). This document is intended to comply with the National Environmental Policy Act of 1969 (NEPA) and its implementing regulations, and NOAA guidelines for compliance with NEPA. As this document focuses on future regional seagrass restoration and injury prevention activities within all of the FKNMS, the discussion of potential positive and negative impacts on the biological, social, and economic environments will not be site or case specific; instead, they will be general in scope. Therefore, the goal of this PEIS is to describe a range of seagrass restoration techniques, used for both primary and compensatory restoration projects and seagrass injury prevention actions that potentially may be implemented in the FKNMS. The types of seagrass restoration and injury prevention projects proposed in this plan will be implemented with funds collected through natural resource damage assessment (NRDA) settlements for injuries to seagrasses within the FKNMS. The anticipated beneficial and adverse environmental and socioeconomic impacts of each restoration technique are discussed in detail.

1.2 NEED FOR PROPOSED ACTION

The FKNMS contains some of the most extensive seagrass beds in the continental United States. Seagrass beds are an important component of the Florida coral reef tract, the third largest barrier reef system in the world. In 1990, Congress recognized the significance of this area when it designated the area as a National Marine Sanctuary, by means of the Florida Keys National Marine Sanctuary and Protection Act (FKNMSPA) (see Figure 1-1). The FKNMSPA was later incorporated into subsequent reauthorizations of the National Marine Sanctuaries Act (NMSA). Implementing seagrass restoration projects in the FKNMS will prevent the injuries from expanding in size or increasing in severity, create the site conditions necessary for the injured areas to recover to pre-incident conditions, and compensate the public and the environment for the services lost from the time of injury until full recovery.

Figure 1-1. Map of the Florida Keys National Marine Sanctuary

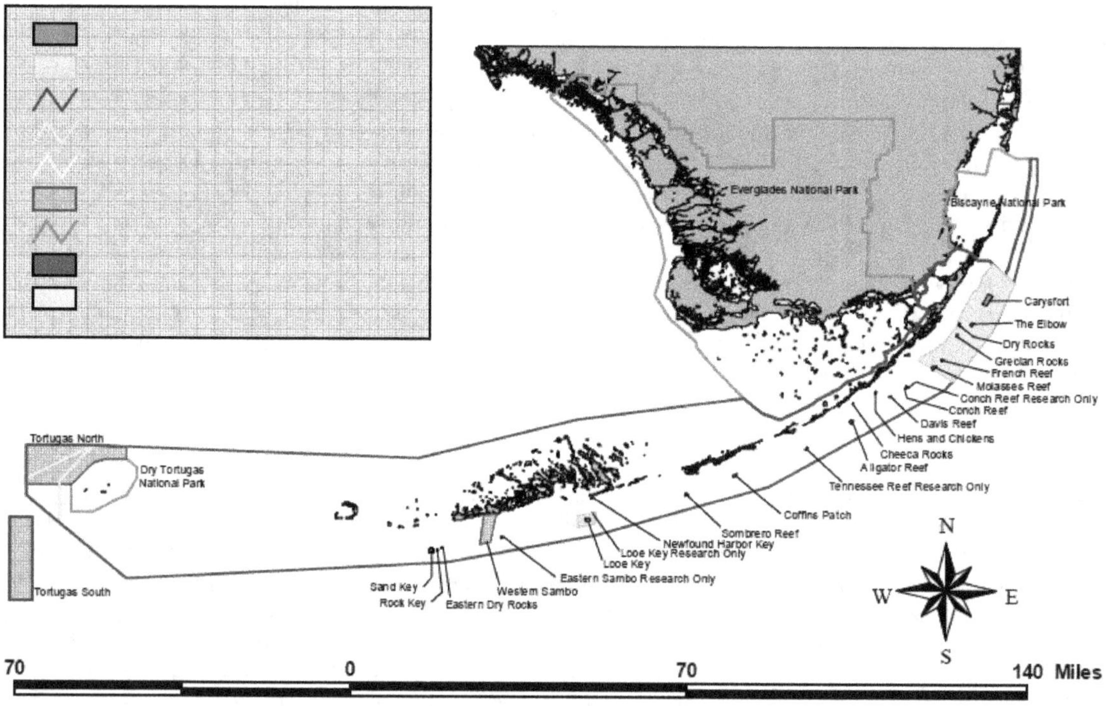

Source: http://www.fknms.nos.noaa.gov

1.3 INTRODUCTION

Healthy seagrass communities serve an important ecological and socioeconomic function in the Florida Keys (FKNMS 1996). The predominant species of seagrasses are *Thalassia testudinum*, *Syringodium filiforme*, and *Halodule wrightii*. From an ecological perspective, seagrass beds are the nurseries for numerous species of fish and invertebrates. In turn, the viability of the recreational and commercial fishing industries, and the associated service industries, are to some degree, directly or indirectly dependent on healthy seagrass communities. From a physical perspective, seagrass beds are also effective storm surge buffers for the low-lying Keys, thereby reducing property damage during extreme weather events. Seagrasses function as natural filters that reduce the level of sediment in the water (i.e. turbidity). The natural filtration of water by seagrasses is a major contributor to the clearness of the water, a characteristic appreciated by those who live on or visit the Keys. This process also protects other members of the living marine resources community, such as coral reefs, which are vulnerable to eutrophicating substances in turbid water.

Seagrass beds can persist under a wide range of hydrodynamic conditions. The horizontal rhizome and root system is underground, protecting much of seagrass biomass from the elements. The root system grows laterally, sending up short shoots that penetrate the surface. *S. filiforme* and *H. wrightii* have shallow root-rhizome systems and can initiate growth in oxidized, relatively unstable sediments, making them the principle seagrass colonizers in an area. Because *T. testudinum* (see Figure 1-2) builds a thicker root-rhizome system deeper underground, it takes this climax species longer to colonize an area, if water depth and wave energy provide the conditions necessary for its growth (Chiappone 1996).

Figure 1-2. Close-up of *Thalassia testudinum* rhizome

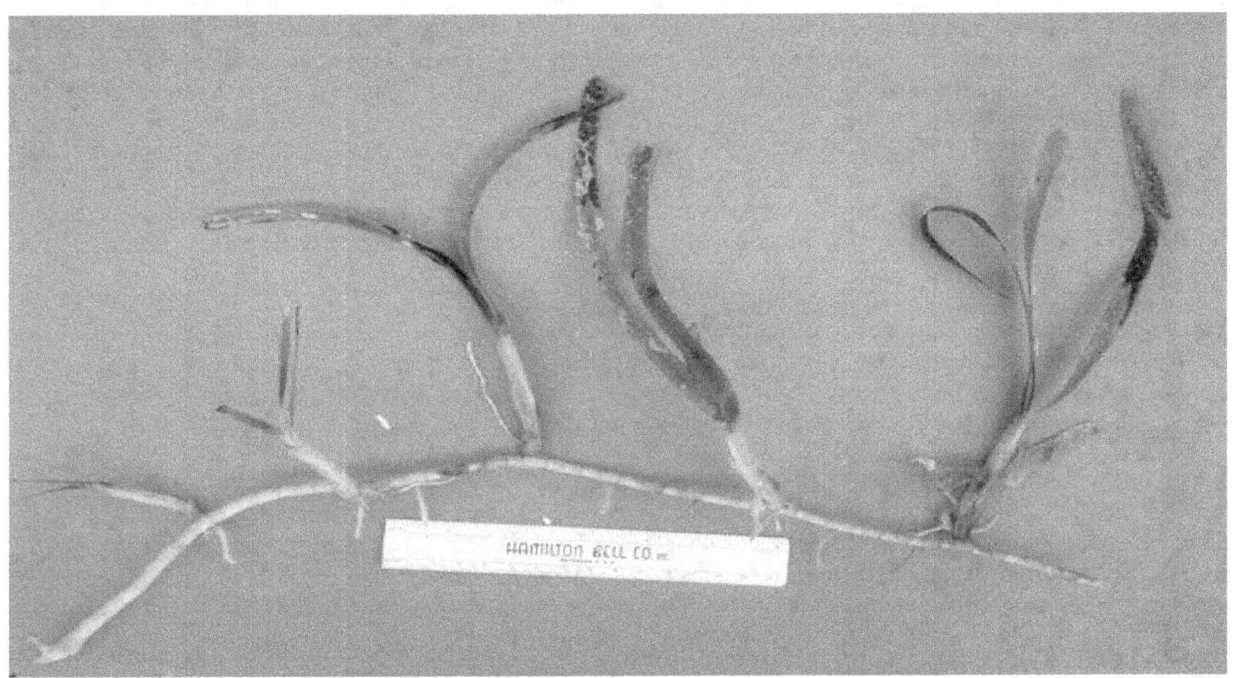

The cumulative impact of vessel groundings has led to a pervasive scarring of seagrass beds throughout the FKNMS (Sargent et al. 1995). In 2001, it was estimated that 677 boat groundings occurred in the FKNMS, with approximately 60-70% of these occurring on seagrass beds.[1] Seagrass injuries in the FKNMS typically include a combination of propeller scars, blowholes, and sediment berms. Propeller scars are formed by the dredging effect of the turning propeller(s) as the boat travels over a shallow bank. The width of a propeller scar varies depending on many factors, including the size of the vessel and the extent to which the propeller is forced into the seagrass bed. Blowholes, another common injury feature, are formed from the concentrated force of propeller wash, either from the grounded vessel attempting to power off the bank or the propeller wash of the salvage vessel pulling the grounded vessel off the bank. The depth and area of the blowholes vary depending on many factors, including size of the vessel, extent of power used to remove the vessel, and type of substrate sediment. Berms, a third common seagrass injury feature, are produced from the sand, coral fragments, and other substrates that typically accumulate around the perimeter of blowholes, thereby burying healthy seagrass.

Restoration is an important step in reducing the cumulative impact of seagrass injuries throughout the Keys. When the underground seagrass rhizome system is damaged and the surrounding sediment altered by structural injuries such as vessel groundings, the seagrass community often has a difficult time reestablishing itself without supplemental restoration efforts.

---

[1] Lt. Bob Currul, Florida Fish and Wildlife Conservation Commission. Personal communication. January, 2002.

The goal of a NRDA is to assess the nature, extent and severity of the injury, implement primary and compensatory restoration to make the environment and public whole, and recover response and damage assessment costs. The Trustees' main seagrass restoration objective for groundings is to conduct feasible, cost-effective, in-kind restoration using the best available techniques to accelerate recovery to the pre-grounding baseline levels. "Primary restoration" refers to restoration activities at the actual grounding site. For seagrasses, "baseline" refers to the level of ecological services that would have been provided but for the incident. These services are directly tied to the type, quality, and density of the seagrass beds. Baseline conditions are typically measured via field assessment techniques in the undisturbed seagrass bordering the grounding site (Fonseca et al. 2000). In many circumstances, without primary restoration the injured seagrass communities are subject to re-disturbance by storms that could slow recovery and/or expand the size of the injury (Whitfield et. al 2002). "Compensatory restoration" refers to a restoration project, typically off-site, that would compensate the public for the lost interim ecological services as a result of the time it takes for the original, "primary" injury to return to baseline conditions. In some instances, compensatory restoration may take the form of preventative projects that seek to reduce the frequency and/or severity of similar grounding incidents. Typically, damages recovered for small compensatory restoration projects would be pooled together for the implementation of a larger compensatory restoration project.

These restoration and injury prevention objectives are in keeping with the goals and policies of the NMSA, the FKNMSPA, the Florida Keys National Marine Sanctuary Management Plan, and the sovereign submerged land policies of the State of Florida. The NMSA, 16 U.S.C.§1443(d)(2) (A), (B), and (C), defines the appropriate uses of recovered damages in order of priority as

> "(A) to restore, replace, or acquire the equivalent of the sanctuary resources that were the subject of the action;
>
> B) to restore degraded sanctuary resources of the national marine sanctuary that was the subject of action, giving priority to sanctuary resources and habitats that are comparable to the sanctuary resources that were the subject of the action; and
>
> (C) to restore degraded sanctuary resources of other national marine sanctuaries."

Amounts recovered for injuries to sanctuary resources lying within the jurisdiction of the State of Florida are used in accordance with the Agreement for the Coordination of Civil Claims between NOAA and the Board of Trustees of the Internal Improvement Trust Fund of the State of Florida.

The restoration activities discussed above will not have a disproportionate or adverse human health or environmental effect on minority and low-income populations in the nearby vicinity or elsewhere, thereby complying with Executive Order 12898, "Federal Actions to Address Environmental Justice in Minority Populations and Low-Income Populations." The low-income and minority populations affected by these injuries and restoration activities are primarily those that live in nearby Monroe County (Key West Chamber of Commerce 1999). The restoration activities discussed in this document serve to return the seagrass banks to their baseline conditions with the effect of providing essential habitat for fish and other marine life on which many members of surrounding minority and low-income communities depend for their livelihood. Restoration will also facilitate natural filtration of the water, which protects nearby coral reefs upon which many minority and low-income persons working in tourism depend. Additionally, restoration will help protect surrounding areas, where many minority and low-income members live, from storm damage. The identification and analysis of disproportionately high environmental and/or human health effects on minority and/or low-income populations was considered from the initial screening phase of the NEPA process through the consideration and communication of all alternatives and associated mitigation techniques.

CHAPTER 2. SEAGRASS RESTORATION ALTERNATIVES

2.1 SEAGRASS RESTORATION SELECTION CRITERIA

Research on various aspects of seagrass ecology and restoration at NOAA's Center for Coastal Fisheries and Habitat Research has been continuous for 20 years (Whitfield et al. 2002; Fonseca 1998). Areas of investigation include development and dissemination of planting techniques, monitoring protocols, and success criteria. In addition, studies have examined light requirements of seagrasses, ecological equivalency of restored beds compared to natural beds, undisturbed systems, and studies regarding the dynamics of seagrass bed pattern and distribution. Emphasis has been placed on transfer of research information to managers, active participation in research projects, and litigation support. The research approach has been to sustain a broad-based program covering a variety of ecological processes that allows the scientists to quickly adapt and respond to changing management concerns and issues.

Based on the Trustees' broad experience with seagrass ecology and restoration, general criteria will be considered for selecting the appropriate restoration alternatives for site-specific seagrass injuries. The following criteria (see Table 2-1) are used to evaluate and select the preferred restoration alternatives. These criteria satisfy the restoration objectives while taking into account technical, environmental, economic, and social factors of the FKNMS and surrounding areas.

Table 2-1. Criteria for Evaluating Seagrass Restoration Options

Criteria	Definition
Technical Feasibility	Likelihood that a given restoration action will work at the site and the technology and management skills exist to implement the restoration action.
Recovery Time	Measures that accelerate or sustain the long-term natural processes important to recovery of the affected resources and/or services injured or lost in the incident.
Additional Injury	Likelihood that the requirements, materials, or implementation of a restoration action minimizes the potential for additional injury.
Aesthetic Acceptability	Restoration alternatives that create substrates and topography that most closely resemble the surrounding habitat and minimize visual degradation.
Site Specific Context	Restoration alternatives are selected depending on the site specific context of environmental conditions at the site including but not limited to location, extent and severity of the injury, hydrological characteristics of the site, seagrass species composition, and other social and resource management concerns.

2.2 SEAGRASS RESTORATION OPTIONS

The following is a list of the most common alternatives for seagrass restoration that are considered prior to the selection of the preferred seagrass restoration alternatives for each site. As most seagrass injury categories are fairly uniform, the techniques listed below are expected to be applicable to virtually all seagrass injury restoration projects. Depending on the scenario, a combination of these alternatives may be most effective. Several other restoration alternatives that are not mentioned, such as mechanical plugging and planting of large sods, have not yet been demonstrated to be successful in the carbonate system of the FKNMS.

2.2.1 No-Action

A no-action alternative may be selected for seagrass injuries that have a high probability of rapid natural recovery or that are logistically or technically incapable of receiving any restoration actions, such as those that occur in very high-energy environments. A no-action alternative relies on natural colonization of seagrass species and natural processes to filling blowholes and propeller scars with sediment. Natural colonization and filling often occurs slowly over many years and may result in conditions that may or may not resemble pre-grounding topography, structure, and function. In contrast, restoration fills in blowholes and propeller scars quickly, and accelerates colonization of seagrass in the injured area. The no-action alternative can have two general outcomes: 1) natural recovery on a longer time scale relative to active restoration alternatives, or 2) further deterioration of the seagrass bed due to the absence of natural recovery. The no-action alternative is most often used for grounding cases in which the Trustees believe there is a low likelihood of secondary injury or injury expansion before natural recovery occurs, or where other social, environmental, or logistical considerations dictate that no-action is the best course (such as in the case of an injury to a *H. wrightii* bed which often recovers quickly on its own). Even if no-action is the selected alternative, compensatory restoration of another injured seagrass area may occur to compensate for the interim service losses. The amount of compensatory restoration necessary to compensate for the interim ecological services lost due to the injury will be determined through a habitat equivalency analysis (HEA) (NOAA 1995b). HEA is a well-established restoration scaling method that has been used in the past by natural resource Trustees to scale a wide range of compensatory restoration projects, including those designed to address injuries to seagrass habitats.

2.2.2 Seagrass Transplants

Planting seagrass in injured areas is known to be an effective way of stabilizing the sediments and decreasing the injury recovery time (Fonseca et al. 1998). Planting faster growing opportunistic species like *H. wrightii* or *S. filiforme* serves as a temporary substitute for the climax species, *T. testudinum*. This temporary substitution is referred to as "modified compressed succession" (Durako and Moffler 1984; Lewis 1987). Depending on the environmental conditions at the restoration site, the selection of seagrass transplants as a preferred restoration alternative will vary. For example, transplants may be selected most frequently at low to moderate energy sites where the probability of transplant loss due to high water velocity is lowest. When best practices are used, seagrass transplants experience a survival rate of 70-80% (Fonseca *et al.* 1998). To date, two small vessel grounding sites have been restored with seagrass transplants in the FKNMS. Though the monitoring cycle (see below) has not been completed, initial monitoring events indicated that both sites exceeded 75% survival after one year. Due to the high risk of hurricanes between August 15 and October 15, no seagrass transplanting will be done during this period.

Potential sources for seagrass transplants include selective removal from healthy seagrass beds located near the injury or from seagrass beds designated previously by the Trustees as semi-permanent donor sites. All efforts will be made to use seagrass transplant stock from areas in the vicinity of the injury to ensure minimal variation in the genetic differences between the resident seagrasses and the transplanted seagrasses. Seagrass transplants will be collected in accordance with all necessary permits and in a manner that ensures that healthy seagrass beds are not degraded. Collection methods have been developed which minimize impact to donor beds of *H. wrightii* and *S. filiforme* and assure rapid recovery after plants have been removed (Fonseca et al. 1998). Specifically, transplant harvesting will entail the collection of numerous, small planting units from within a donor site. This will avoid creating a large hole in the donor bed's standing stock, and decrease the time required for the bed to replenish itself. Sustained injury to donor sites from limited harvesting efforts has been demonstrated to occur for only one of the thirteen species of North American seagrass, *T. testudinum* (Fonseca et al. 1998). As the comparatively faster growing species *H. wrightii* and *S. filiforme* will be harvested for transplants, no adverse effects on donor sites are expected. No negative impacts to vessel navigation or the ecological health of neighboring seagrass communities are anticipated from seagrass transplant collection and insertion, and there is no evidence that any invasive or exotic species have occupied donor sites. See section 2.2.4 for a description of seagrass transplant spacing.

Monitoring events will assess transplant and natural re-colonization via measures of planting unit (PU) survival, shoot density, aerial coverage, and documentation with video transects. The execution and

6

application of the monitoring effort is adapted from "Guidelines for the Conservation and Restoration of Seagrasses in the United States and Adjacent Waters", available at: http://shrimp.bea nmfs.gov/library/digital.html, under "Appendices", pages 207-220, or http://www.cop noaa.gov/pubs/das/das12 html. Briefly, the monitoring data will be used to determine if successful establishment of transplanted seagrass has occurred and if it is on an appropriate recovery trajectory. If not, these data will be used to plan and execute remedial restoration. The success criteria are:

1) whether planted material has a minimum of one rhizome apical per PU,
2) a PU survival rate of 75% at the end of Year 1. If it is determined that less than 75% survival has occurred by the end of Year 1, then remedial planting should occur during the next available planting period to bring the percentage survival rate to the minimum standard by the next monitoring survey, and
3) the measured growth rate of bottom coverage from either direct quadrat surveys or video-based assessment (p. 220 of above weblink; Braun-Blanquet assessment). The growth rate should be considered successful if, starting after Year 1, the planted pioneering species of seagrass in the restoration sites is projected with 95% statistical confidence to achieve complete bottom coverage to pre-injury levels of shoot density within the five year monitoring period for original plantings. If this criterion is not met, then remedial planting should occur during the next available planting period.

Videotaping is also performed to provide an unambiguous record of the status of the restoration. This is particularly valuable to parties not familiar with seagrass systems and interpretation of statistical data.

Additionally, the seagrass immediately surrounding the injury site (e.g. "reference site") will also be monitored. This action will be taken to determine if background impacts not related to the restoration (those that cannot be controlled nor affected through a mid-course correction), such as poor water quality or disease, may affect transplant and natural re-colonization of the restoration site. The purpose of monitoring the reference site is not to compare its coverage and density to that of the restoration site as recovery of the restoration site will take place over a longer time horizon than the duration of monitoring. Monitoring of reference sites will include documentation of percent cover by Braun Blanquet quadrat analysis.

2.2.3 Bird Stakes

In most areas of the FKNMS, seagrasses are nutrient limited.[2] As such, when vessel injuries disturb the sediment nutrient reservoir, the ability of seagrasses to re-colonize is more difficult. A method of fertilization that utilizes the nutrient composition of bird feces deposited from birds roosting on stakes (hereinafter referred to as "bird stakes" or "stakes", see Figure 2-1) has been documented to be an effective treatment to facilitate colonization of seagrasses into disturbed sediments and/or faster growth of seagrass transplants (Fourqurean et al. 1992a; Fourqurean et al. 1992b; Fourqurean et al. 1995; Kenworthy et al. 2000). Bird stakes are preferable to fertilizer spikes in water depths of up to 1.5 meters, as they do not need to be continually replaced.

To be effective, bird staking requires that bird feces reach the seafloor in concentrated doses for as long as the stakes are in place. Water depths of 1.5 meters or less at mean high tide are generally considered ideal for bird staking. With water depths greater than 1.5 meters, the effect of dilution on the feces is believed to reduce the effective strength of the fertilizer. Depending on how water depth changes over the injury area, the length of each stake may vary slightly in order to maintain approximately 0.25 m elevation above the

---

[2] Although many areas of the Keys suffer from high levels of nitrogen loading from leaking septic tanks and other non-point sources, the relatively diffuse spread of these nutrients are not as effective in fostering seagrass recovery as a concentrated release of nitrogen and phosphorous fertilizer from bird stakes (Fourqueran et al. 1995).

high water level. Research has demonstrated that if left on site too long, bird stakes may cause a communal shift of seagrass species from *T. testudinum* to *H. wrightii* (Powell et al. 1989). Thus, bird stakes are removed after approximately 75% survival coalescence is reached, which is usually after 18 months. A detailed review of bird stake construction and placement requirements are available in published guidelines (Fonseca et al. 1998; Kenworthy et al. 2000). There is no evidence that proper use of bird stakes impairs local water quality. Deployment in areas of less than 1.5-meter water depth ensures that the majority of the feces reach the seafloor in concentrated doses, precluding the nutrients from fueling harmful algal blooms.

Several species of birds have been observed using bird stakes at both research and restoration sites in the FKNMS. The most common species that have been recorded using bird stakes are double crested cormorants (*Phalacrocorax auritus*), least terns (*Sterna antillarum*), royal terns (*Sterna maxima*), brown pelicans (*Pelicanus occidentalis*), magnificent frigate birds (*Fregata magnificens*), and great blue herons (*Ardea herodias*). The cormorants are the primary target for roosting and the most frequently observed species using the bird stakes. There is no evidence that the bird stakes affect populations or distribution of bird species in the FKNMS.

In most instances, bird stakes will accompany seagrass transplants. This decision is based on factors including the exposure of the site to wave action, density of fast-growing species in the undisturbed side populations, and injury substrate composition. Depending on the site-specific context of a case, portions of a scar may receive only stakes, while a different portion receives stakes and seagrass transplants. However, at injury locations with a high density of fast-growing species (e.g. *H. wrightii*), the insertion of bird stakes alone may be sufficient to encourage colonization.

The possibility for bird stakes interfering with vessel navigation is low, as bird stakes will be positioned in shallow water areas that should be avoided by vessels. In areas of high vessel traffic, additional steps may be taken to minimize the possibility of boaters confusing stakes for public or privately placed navigational aids. This may involve the placement of additional bird stakes at either end of the prop scar to create a stake barrier. Other methods may include the use of educational signs and reflective tape on the stakes to reduce the possibility that boaters will confuse the stakes for a new channel passage. Bird stakes will be removed promptly from the site as soon as recovery is determined to be well underway or at the end of the allocated monitoring period time as detailed in the restoration plan. See section 2.2.4 for a description of bird stake spacing.

Figure 2-1. Bird Stake Schematic

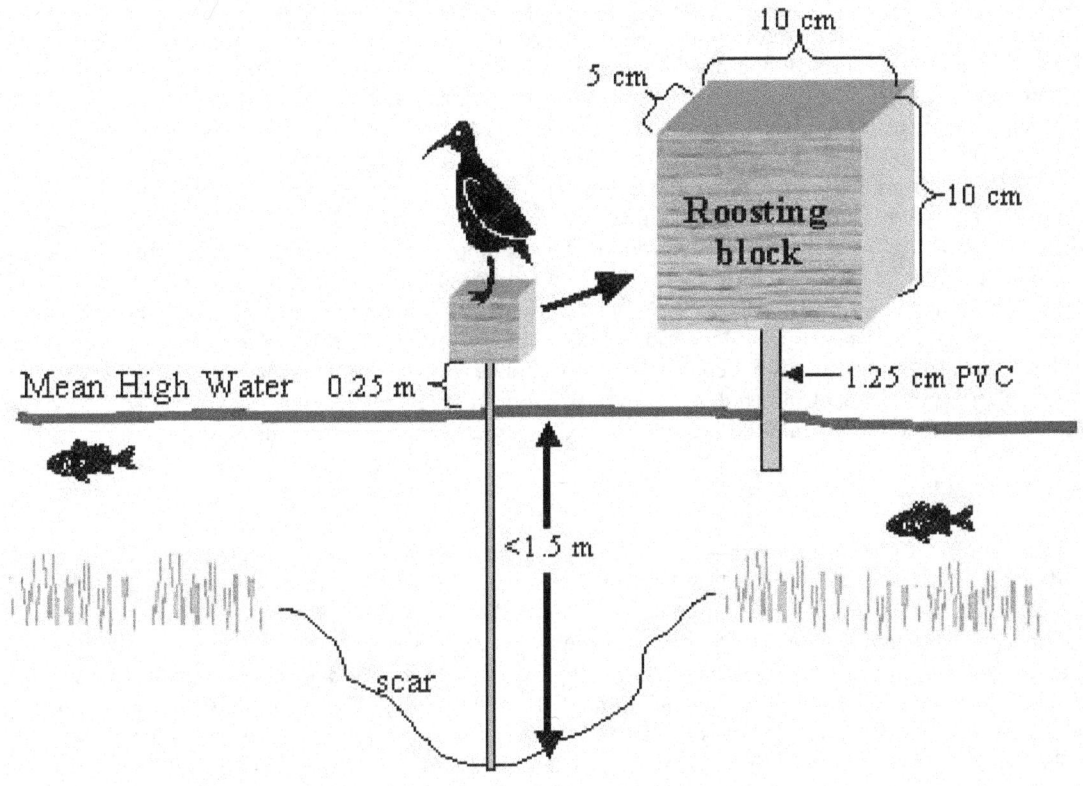

2.2.4 Fertilizer Spikes

Bird stakes are the preferred technique for ensuring regular release of fertilizer over an area of approximately 3 square meters below the stake. However, in situations where bird stakes are inappropriate, such as in water depths over 1.5 meters, the use of chemical fertilizer spikes is another alternative to enhance seagrass colonization of the injury area. A broad review article published by Worm et al. (2000) documents that the benefits of in-situ nutrient enrichment through fertilizer spikes have been demonstrated in numerous studies to be an effective method for seagrass restoration. These in-situ nutrient enrichment studies have shown that fertilizer spikes deliver a high load of phosphorus, the main limiting nutrient for seagrasses growing on carbonate sediments in the FKNMS (Worm et al. 2000). Fertilizer spikes will naturally biodegrade in approximately three to four months, at which time, depending on the status of the restoration project, additional fertilizer spikes may be inserted. The placement of fertilizer spikes will follow guidelines for seagrass transplants as detailed below, with no more than one spike placed directly adjacent to each transplant unit. The advantages of fertilizer spikes are: 1) they deliver a concentrated dose of nutrients in a small area that directly benefits individual planting units; 2) they are easier to deploy than encapsulated fertilizers, a significant advantage in coarse, firm sediments; 3) they are suitable for water depths greater than 1.5 meters; and 4) they are a viable fertilizer enhancement alternative when bird stakes are inappropriate due to hazards to navigation or risk of vandalism.

The number of seagrass transplants and stakes/spikes required for propeller scars is determined according to the following general guidelines. These guidelines are subject to modification based on site-specific injury characteristics and the professional judgment of Trustee restoration experts. The longer axis of a propscar is defined as its length and the shorter axis is its width. For propscars less than 1.5 m in width, only a single row of stakes/spikes and seagrass transplants is used. The stakes/spikes and transplants are inserted in the middle of the scar and the row runs the length of the injury. The first stake is inserted at the beginning of the scar (at 0.0m along its length). Additional stakes are then placed along the injury with 2.0 m between each stake. Thus, for example, a scar that is 10 m in length would have six stakes. Three seagrass transplants are inserted between the first two stakes, at distances of 0.5 m, 1.0 m, and 1.5 m along the scar. Seagrasses are not transplanted directly under the stakes. This planting pattern is repeated for the length of the injury. A 10 m scar would require 15 seagrass transplants. For scars between 1.5 and 2.0 m in width, two rows are inserted. The first, a row of stakes and planting units as described above, is inserted 0.5m into the width of the scar. The second row is composed of only seagrass planting units and is inserted 1.0m into the width of the scar. Thus, the two rows divide the width of the scar into thirds. Additional seagrass transplants are placed in the second row instead of stakes (resulting in a row of 16 transplants for a 10 m scar). This general pattern is maintained for wider propscars, blowholes, and berms. Additionally, the perimeter of blowholes is staked at 2.0 m intervals. Over time, stakes/spikes may be re-positioned and additional seagrass transplants inserted as necessary during monitoring events.

2.2.5 Sediment Fill

Blowholes are a common seagrass injury associated with vessel groundings. In general, the size of the grounded vessel and degree of propeller force used by the grounded vessel or the salver to remove the vessel correlates to the size of the blowhole. The filling of blowholes, or in some circumstances wide propeller scars, is a rapid way of returning the seafloor to its original grade. In general, any excavation with an escarpment (i.e. drop-off) greater than 20 cm deep at the perimeter is considered a potential candidate for filling. The focus of this alternative is to stabilize the substrate as soon as possible after an incident to prevent further deterioration from erosion and to prepare the area for colonization by neighboring or transplanted seagrasses. When this alternative is determined to be most appropriate, sediment fill, (e.g. 0.25 inch limestone pea rock) initially garnered from quarries, will be transported to the site and directly placed in the designated injury areas. It is expected that fine sediments from the local area will eventually fill the interstitial spaces of the pea gravel. No visual impairment will occur and many of the repairs will be indistinguishable from surrounding substrate within a short period of time. All operations will conform to engineering specifications and comply with federal and state permits, including an Army Corps of Engineers (ACOE) permit and a *de minimus* permit from the Florida Department of Environmental Protection to allow seagrass restoration (stake, plant and fill) in Sanctuary waters.

2.2.6 Sediment Tubes

An additional seagrass restoration technique involves the placement of biodegradable sediment-filled fabric mesh tubes (referred hereinafter as "sediment tubes") inside of the trench created by propeller scars or on top of sediment fill in blowholes. These sediment tubes are effective in reducing erosion rates in injuries and fostering conditions suitable for natural re-colonization of the injured area by neighboring seagrasses and growth of seagrass transplants. Sediment tubes as a restoration technique may be appropriate in a variety of circumstances, including but not limited to, propeller scar injury excavations and small blowholes or when blowhole fill requires a protective barrier to reduce erosional forces. As such, the design of tubes will be slightly tailored to the specific geometry of each injury. Most of the tube deployments will be comprised of two tubes laid atop one another, capping the sediment fill placed in the excavation. The tubes replace the 10 cm above-grade topping of sediment fill required when tubes are not used. If seagrass transplants are also required, *H. wrightii* transplants will be planted in the tubes. Depending on the specific context of the injury, sediment tubes may be used in combination with any other restoration technique to expedite stabilization and recovery of the injured area. A primary advantage of using sediment tubes is their ability to mitigate erosional forces that may otherwise act to remove or displace the sediment fill. Depending on the specific site conditions of an injury site, it is forseeable that restoration actions may include a combination of fill, tubes, and berm redistribution in order to most effectively stabilize the site.

2.2.7 Berm Redistribution

Blowhole and large propeller scar injuries often create berms of sediment surrounding the injury site. In some circumstances, where the displaced fill is directly adjacent to the injury site and easily accessible, restoration experts may be able to return the displaced fill back into the injury by either raking or water-dredging, or some combination of the two. However, this is only an alternative when doing so will not injure any seagrass that may still be living below the berm. Redistribution of fill is an immediate, low-cost, and low-risk restoration action that advances stabilization of the injury site and recovery of the area previously covered by sediment. In addition, redistribution of fill may minimize injury to adjacent seagrass beds covered by the berms created by the incident.

2.2.8 Sod Replacement

When appropriate, large chunks of seagrasses with intact rhizomes that were dislodged as a result of an injury may be placed back into a shallow propscar injury or blowhole. This alternative is suitable for shallow blowholes or propscars where additional sediment fill is not needed for the replaced seagrass to continue to thrive once replaced. This restoration technique expedites recovery of the injured sites, resulting in direct and indirect ecological and socioeconomic benefits associated with healthy seagrass ecosystems. For groundings that produce chunks of seagrass with intact rhizomes and result in injury features that do not require sediment fill, sod replacement will be done immediately after injury assessment to maximize the chance of sod survival.

2.2.9 Exclusion Cages

When injuries to seagrass beds occur near coral reefs, it is especially difficult for the seagrass to reestablish itself after restoration. A large variety of herbivores live in or frequent coral reefs and thus put abnormally high grazing pressure on nearby seagrass. Uninjured, well-established seagrass beds can sustain this pressure, but new transplants are quickly grazed to the point where they cannot sustain themselves because they are planted as smaller fragments or units, which are not integrated clonally as are plants growing in an established meadow. However, research has shown that exclusion cages placed around new transplants for three to four months allow the beds to establish themselves to the point where they are sustainable after the cages are removed (Fonseca et al. 1994). Each exclusion cage must also be securely fastened to the substrate so that it does not become detached. This is particularly important in areas where cages are exposed to storm waves, ground swells and other high-energy events.

2.3 PROPOSED ACTIONS

In most seagrass restoration projects, a combination of one or more of the alternatives presented will be identified as the preferred alternative(s) in an injury-specific restoration plan. Trustees with expertise in seagrass restoration ecology and first-hand experience with the grounding site select the proposed preferred alternative. Berm redistribution and sod replacement will occur at the time of injury assessment, if warranted. Typically, seagrass transplants will be accompanied with bird stakes if the water depth is less than 1.5 meters or fertilizer spikes if water depth is greater than 1.5 meters. Exclusion cages will be placed over seagrass transplants in areas close to coral reefs. In addition, if the site-specific conditions warrant sediment fill for blowholes or sediment tubes for wide propeller scars or blowholes, seagrass transplants and bird stakes will be inserted after sediment placement activities. Finally, if it is determined that the grounding site is likely to recover rapidly or primary restoration is not appropriate due to other reasons, the no-action alternative may be assigned for part or all of the injury site. Table 2-

2 summarizes the alternatives available, the conditions under which they may be chosen, and the ultimate results of their applications.

Table 2-2. Seagrass Restoration Alternative Matrix/Comparison

ALTERNATIVE	SITE CONDITION	RESULT
No Action: Leaving the injury untouched.	Chosen for injuries where there is a relatively small likelihood of secondary injury before natural recovery occurs, or where any restoration is considered too difficult to undertake due to high-energy conditions.	• Natural recovery occurs on a longer time scale relative to restoration activities. OR • Further deterioration of the seagrass bed occurs due to ineffective natural recovery.
Seagrass Transplants: Planting seagrass (*S. filiforme* and *H. wrightii*) taken from donor sites in injured areas including berms, blowholes and/or propscars.	Often selected at low to moderate energy sites, where the probability of transplant loss due to high water velocity is lowest.	• Stabilization of sediments decreases injury recovery time. • Planting faster growing opportunistic species like *H. wrightii* or *S. filiforme* serves as a temporary substitute for the climax species, *T. testudinum*.
Bird Stakes: Insertion of stakes upon which birds roost, dropping their feces on and thus fertilizing seagrass beds. Inserted into berms, blowholes and/or propscars.	Used on seagrass beds in water depths of 1.5 meters or less (mean high water).	• Bird feces reach the seagrass floor for as long as the stakes are in place. • Colonization of seagrasses into disturbed sediments is facilitated and/or seagrass transplants grow at a faster rate than natural recovery. • Fertilizer is released regularly over an area of approximately 3 square meters below the stake
Fertilizer Spikes: Insertion of chemical fertilizer spikes that release fertilizer into the sediments of replanted seagrass beds over a period of 3-4 months. Inserted into berms, blowholes and/or propscars.	Used on replanted seagrass beds when water depths are greater than 1.5 meters or when bird stakes are inappropriate due to hazards to navigation or risk of vandalism.	• Colonization of seagrasses into disturbed sediments is facilitated and/or seagrass transplants grow at a faster rate. • A concentrated dose of nutrients is delivered in a small area that directly benefits individual planting units.
Sediment Fill: Filling of blowholes or wide propeller scars with sediment similar to that of the surrounding area.	Used for injuries greater than 20 cm deep.	• The seafloor is rapidly returned to its original grade. • The substrate is stabilized quickly after an incident to prevent further deterioration from erosion and to prepare the area for colonization by neighboring or transplanted seagrasses.
Sediment Tubes: Placement of biodegradable sediment-filled fabric mesh tubes inside the trench of a propscar or blowhole.	Often used in narrow excavations (such as propscars) deeper than 20 cm or to cap fill placed in larger blowholes in high-energy environments.	• Erosion rates are reduced. • Conditions are made more suitable for natural re-colonization of the injured area by neighboring seagrasses and growth of transplants is fostered.

Table 2-2. Seagrass Restoration Alternative Matrix/Comparison (continued)

ALTERNATIVE	SITE CONDITION	RESULT
Berm Redistribution: Returning displaced fill back into the injury.	Undertaken when it is believed that doing so will not cause more harm by damaging live seagrass below the berm.	• Stabilization of the injury site and recovery of the area previously covered by sediment is enhanced.
Sod Replacement: Replacement of large chunks of seagrasses with intact rhizomes back into a shallow propscar injury or blowhole.	Used in shallow injuries where intact seagrass chunks can be found	• Regrowth of dislodged sod. • Stabilization of the injury site and recovery of the area.
Exclusion Cages: Enclosing seagrass transplants with a cage to prevent it from being overgrazed.	Used in restoration sites located near coral reefs.	• Allows seagrass beds to reestablish themselves to the point where they are not overgrazed when the cages are removed.

CHAPTER 3. AFFECTED ENVIRONMENT

This chapter provides background information on the potentially affected environments associated with seagrass restoration projects in the FKNMS. As this PEIS is regional in scope, emphasis is placed on presenting a range of affected resources over the entire FKNMS region. Given the size of the FKNMS and uncertainty with regard to where exactly each restoration project will occur, by necessity, a site-specific discussion of potential restoration sites and specific environments affected is not possible.

3.1 LOCATION AND AREA USES

Located almost completely within Monroe County, the FKNMS consists of approximately 9,500 km^2 of coastal and oceanic waters and submerged lands. Uses of the general area include diving, fishing, snorkeling and boating. The FKNMS holds not only recreational and commercial value, but also scientific, historical, ecological and educational value (NOAA 2000; NOAA 2002). Many scientists view the area as a living laboratory in which numerous scientific studies and other research are being conducted (UNEP/IUCN 1988; NOAA 2002). Many marine species found within the FKNMS's boundaries hold commercial or recreational value, including spiny lobster, grouper, mackerel, dolphin, snapper, hogfish, tarpon, pompano, jack, and bonefish (NOAA 1995a). Although fishing for these species in portions of the FKNMS is allowed, certain restrictions apply, such as not using harmful fishing methods (e.g. wire fish traps) (UNEP/IUCN 1988; NOAA 2002).

Seagrass banks are located on both the Atlantic Ocean and Gulf of Mexico sides of the FKNMS, encompassing approximately 1,860 square kilometers (Figure 3-1). *H. wrightii, S. filiforme* and *T. testudinum* can be found in mixed beds or alone at depths of between 1 and 20 meters where suitable substrate and favorable physical conditions exist. *H. wrightii* tolerates surface exposure better than the other species, and usually grows in shallower water. *T. testudinum* forms extensive mature meadows, usually at depths of less than 10 to 12 meters, but can be found at greater depths in less density. Between 12 and 15 meters, *S. filiforme* replaces *T. testudinum*, and *H. wrightii* is dominant below 15 meters, but does not form dense stands (NOAA 1996b). Table 3-1 provides a description of the dominant transport processes and benthic community composition for various regions within the FKNMS.

Figure 3-1. Benthic Map of the Florida Keys

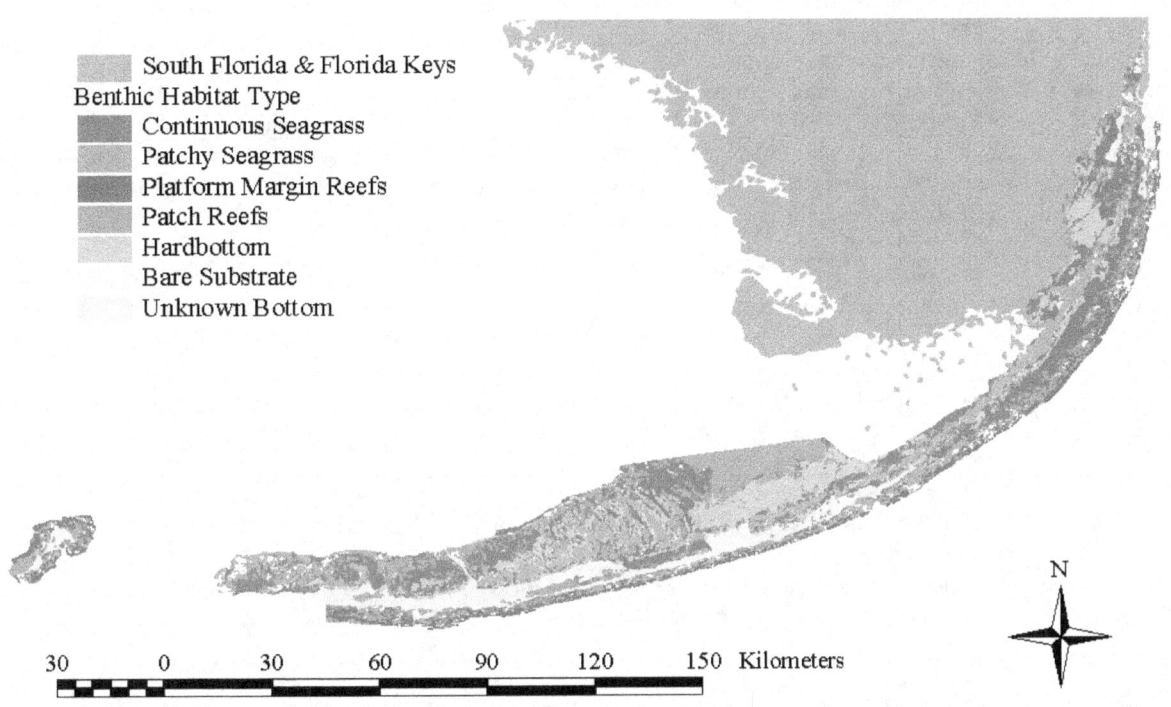

South Florida & Florida Keys
Benthic Habitat Type
Continuous Seagrass
Patchy Seagrass
Platform Margin Reefs
Patch Reefs
Hardbottom
Bare Substrate
Unknown Bottom

Source: FMRI/NOAA 1998

Table 3-1. Benthic Chart of the Florida Keys

AREA	DESCRIPTION AND DOMINANT TRANSPORT PROCESSES	BENTHIC COMMUNITIES
Florida Bay	Semi-isolated, shallow basins and banks dominated by discharge from Taylor Slough; restricted circulation and relatively high variability in physical-chemical parameters.	Mostly seagrass, but also bare sand patches, and occasional exposed hard-bottom substrate; benthic habitats vary considerably across the bay.
Nearshore Middle Keys	Shallow, unconfined, large tidal passes dominated by Florida Bay water with wind-driven circulation and tides.	Mostly seagrass, particularly in channels, but also extensive areas of low-relief hard-bottom habitats within 1 km of shore.
Nearshore Lower Keys	Shallow backcountry, small tidal passes transporting water from the southwest Florida shelf and dominated by wind-driven circulation and tides.	Mostly seagrass, bare sand, and algae, but also extensive areas of low-relief hard-bottom habitats.
Offshore Upper Keys	Area confined by reef tract and dominated by Florida current frontal eddies.	Mostly seagrass and sand, but extensive patch reef and bank reef areas in Hawk Channel and along reef tract; most extensive reef development in the Florida Keys.
Offshore Middle Keys	Area confined by reef tract and dominated by onshore currents and tidally driven exchange with Florida Bay.	Mostly seagrass and sand areas with very poor reef development offshore.
Offshore Lower Keys	Area confined by reef tract and dominated by wind-driven circulation in Hawk Channel and offshore gyres.	Mostly seagrass and bare sand, but extensive areas of hard-bottom with moderate patch reef and bank development.
Marquesas	Unconfined area dominated by southwest Florida shelf water and gyre migrations from the Florida current.	Mostly seagrass with very poor development of reefs and lack of extensive low-relief hard-bottom habitats.
Dry Tortugas	Deeper unconfined area dominated by variability in the Gulf of Mexico Loop Current and the Tortugas Gyre.	Mixture of seagrass, sand, and hard-bottom areas; moderate shallow-water reef development near islands.

Source: Chiappone 1996

Seagrass beds are highly productive, faunally rich ecosystems that provide food, protection and nesting sites for many species of fishes, amphibians, reptiles, birds, and mammals. Seventy to 90 percent of the harvested species in the Gulf depend on seagrass beds during at least part of their life cycle. Dense seagrass also provide protected habitat for a wide variety of juvenile fishes and invertebrates (NOAA 1996b).

Research has shown no common trends in the FKNMS in seagrass health in terms of cover or community composition. However, because the length of time seagrass beds take to eutrophicate is on the order of decades, and the interaction man has with the natural dynamics of these systems is not completely understood, it is difficult to say with certainty whether seagrass beds in the FKNMS are growing or shrinking (Fourqurean et al. 2001).

3.2 SURROUNDING LAND USE

The terrestrial area surrounding potential seagrass restoration projects incorporates all of the Florida Keys (primarily Monroe County) and a variety of land-use activities. The Florida Keys has many different categories of zoning for residential and commercial development and environmental protection. The approximately 480 marinas and boat launches that provide access to the FKNMS serve as gateways for many visitors (Monroe County 1995). Table 3-2 reflects the most recent (1991) distribution of terrestrial land use activities in Monroe County. The data does not include water bodies or offshore islands. A high percentage of land (33.7%) has been set aside for conservation.

Table 3-2. Monroe County Existing Land Use (in acres)

	Upper Keys	Middle Keys	Lower Keys	Total	% of Total
Single-Family	3,391	2,037.0	2,950.9	8,378.9	13.7%
Mobile Homes	618.9	130.8	313.1	1,062.8	1.7%
Multi-Family	391.6	220.9	25.2	637.7	1.0%
Mixed Residential	201.5	158.3	351.1	710.9	1.2%
Residential Subtotal	4,603.0	2,547	3,640.3	10,790.3	17.6%
General Commercial	462.1	276.6	255.4	994.1	1.6%
Commercial Fishing	10.7	84.6	151.8	247.1	0.4%
Tourist Commercial	421.1	460.5	147.3	1,028.9	1.7%
Commercial Subtotal	893.9	821.7	554.5	2,270.1	3.7%
Industrial	81.7	55.2	377.9	514.8	0.8%
Agricultural/Maricultural	0.0	41.9	0.0	41.9	0.1%
Education	65.8	31.7	8.9	106.4	0.2%
Institutional	46.2	37.3	32.8	116.3	0.2%
Public Buildings/Grounds	11.3	32.6	16.9	60.8	0.1%
Public Facilities	36.1	446.2	56.8	539.1	0.9%
Military	0.0	0.0	3,288.7	3,288.7	5.4%
Historic	0.0	0.0	0.5	0.5	0.0%
Recreation	351.2	940.7	499.4	1,791.3	2.9%
Conservation	11,542.6	623.1	8,530	20,695.7	33.7%
Vacant	5,123.1	2,882.5	13,121.6	21,127.2	34.4%
Total	22,754.9	8,459.9	30,128.3	61,343.1	100%
Percent of Total	37.1%	13.8%	49.1%	100%	

Source: Monroe County Board of Commissioners 1993.

3.3 CLIMATE

The Florida Keys are considered a subtropical zone characterized by warm, humid summers, with abundant rainfall and generally warm, moderately dry winters. The average annual temperature is 26 degrees Celsius ($^{\circ}$C), with an average low of 21°C in January, and an average high of 30°C in July. The average annual rainfall is 100 centimeters. The heaviest precipitation occurs during the summer and early to mid-autumn. Winds average 19 kilometers per hour. The prevailing wind direction is from the east-southeast during the summer and from the northeast during the winter. Winds are typically strongest during the winter months and calmest in the spring and autumn. The hurricane season is from June to November, with the peak threat existing from mid-August to late October (NWS 1994).

3.4 AIR QUALITY

National Ambient Air Quality Standards (NAAQS) have been set for six "criteria" pollutants (sulfur dioxide, carbon monoxide, ozone, nitrogen oxides, lead, and particulate matter). The USEPA has recently replaced the 1–hour ozone standard with an 8-hour standard, and the NAAQS for particulate matter has been set for air particles less than 2.5 microns in size. The problems associated with carbon monoxide and particulate matter are usually related to localized conditions, such as congested traffic intersections or construction activities. The other criteria pollutants are associated with regional problems that result from the interactions of pollutants from a great number of widely dispersed sources (e.g., a large city containing many stationary and mobile sources). The Florida Department of Environmental Protection (FDEP) monitors the concentrations of the criteria pollutants and, where necessary, is responsible for developing State Implementation Plans (SIPs) to ensure that the national standards are achieved and maintained. Areas within the state that fail to meet the NAAQS are designated as "non-attainment areas" and are potentially subject to regulatory enforcement. Potential seagrass restoration sites are located in Monroe County, which is classified as being in complete attainment of the NAAQS.

3.5 NOISE

Depending on the location of the restoration sites, noise will be generated from a variety of sources. It is expected that for most restoration sites, the only primary noise sources directly attributable to the restoration will be motor vessels traveling to the project site and any other mechanical equipment that may be required (e.g. pumps, compressors, generators).

3.6 GEOLOGY

The dominant geological feature in the FKNMS is the Florida Plateau, a large carbonate platform composed of carbonate marine sediments approximately 7,000 meters in thickness. The plateau includes all of Florida and the adjacent continental shelves of the Gulf of Mexico and the Atlantic Ocean. The platform has been an area of shallow water carbonate deposition since at least the Jurassic period (136 to 190 million years ago). Sediments accumulating in the area for 150 million years have been structurally modified by subsidence and sea level rise (Continental Shelf Associates 1990). Sea level fluctuations attributed to glacial effects are largely responsible for the present morphology of the area. Sea level dropped by 15 to 30 meters during the Wisconsin glacial period, exposing the entire platform to marine and subareal erosion. Sea level began to rise again approximately 6,000 years ago, flooding the area and forming the current physiographic character of the region. It is expected that the substrate at most restoration sites will be a combination of dense carbonate sand and mud, with significant amounts of larger pieces of broken shells and coral skeletons. At most sites, the combination of the seagrass rhizome and root mat yields a very dense, packed substrate that is difficult to disturb (Zieman 1982).

3.7 WATER QUALITY

Numerous factors exist that influence seagrass distribution and relative abundance. Some of the most identifiable include temperature, salinity, water depth, sediment depth, wave and tidal currents, water column transparency, and nutrient loading (Fonseca 1990; Kenworthy and Haunert 1991; Zieman 1982; Zieman and Zieman 1989). If seagrasses can exist within the other above specified tolerance criteria, light penetration is the most important factor affecting their growth and survival. In fact, it is possible to predict seagrass growth and survival from the known levels of certain key water-quality parameters affecting light transmission (Dennison et al. 1993; Gallegos and Kenworthy 1996). Six frequently measured water quality parameters correlated with the growth and survival of seagrass are: 1) total suspended solids, 2) chlorophyll a, 3) dissolved inorganic nitrogen, 4) dissolved inorganic phosphorus, 5) Secchi depth, and 6) light attenuation. Two of these parameters, total suspended solids and chlorophyll a, are directly responsible for water column transparency to light (i.e., turbidity), while dissolved inorganic nitrogen and phosphorus act indirectly on light attenuation by stimulating algae growth. Secchi depth and light attenuation are quantitative measures of the effect the other four parameters have on water transparency (Kenworthy and Haunert 1991; Kenworthy and Fonseca 1996).

3.8 PHYSICAL PARAMETERS

FKNMS is part of an open-ended environment influenced by the Caribbean Sea, Gulf of Mexico, and Florida Bay. A complex system of currents runs through these bodies of water. Wind-driven currents are characteristic of the Florida Keys because shallow depths prevail throughout the area (Schomer and Drew 1982). Recent studies using satellite tracked surface drifters indicate a net southerly flow from the Gulf of Mexico to the Florida reef tract through western Florida Bay that varies with season, stronger in the winter (3 to 4 cm/s) and weaker in summer (1 to 2 cm/s) (Lee et al. 1998).

Tides in the Florida Keys generally exhibit two highs and two lows of uneven amplitude (height) per tidal day (Schomer and Drew 1982). The tidal range decreases from Fowey Rocks in the upper Florida Keys to Sand Key offshore of Key West. Tides in the lower Keys area vary approximately 0.3 to 0.6 meters. The highest observed water level in the area was recorded at Coupon Bight near Big Pine Key at 0.9 meters above the mean lower low water (MLLW) level in 1974; the lowest observed tide was measured in the Big Pine Key Viaduct, Pine Channel, at -0.3 meters below MLLW in 1974 (NOAA 1998).

Tidal currents reverse in direction with the ebb and flow of tides. These currents show a slight westward component, especially in the middle and lower Florida Keys (Enos 1997; Smith 1991). Tidal current velocities range from 5 to 15 centimeters per second, but velocities as high as 130 centimeters per second have been recorded. However, these tidal components are usually offset by wind. As mentioned above, recent studies indicate that there is a long-term net flow from Florida Bay/Gulf of Mexico to the Atlantic Ocean (Pitts 1994; Smith 1994).

3.9 BIOLOGICAL RESOURCES

3.9.1 Seagrass

The seagrass meadows of south Florida constitute one of the most important natural resources in the state (Iverson and Bittaker 1986; Fourqurean et al. 2000). They have high natural rates of primary productivity that is greatest during the summer (Zieman and Zieman 1989). These high rates of growth result in large leaf canopies that serve as an important food source and critical habitat for important commercial and recreational fish and shellfish species. Bank-top *T. testudinum* in Florida Bay has been found to support higher faunal densities than shallow seagrasses elsewhere in south Florida (Sheridan 1997).

Three dominant species of seagrasses found in high salinity, open coastal waters are turtle grass (*T. testudinum*), manatee grass (*S. filiforme*) and shoal grass (*H. wrightii*). The first two species are usually associated with stable, near-marine salinities (20-36%), open coastal water, and subtropical to tropical temperatures. Shoal grass is found in more estuarine conditions, but also forms dense stands in open coastal, high-salinity regions and in areas of high water movement, or in tidal flats where it is subject to exposure. All three species have high heat tolerance and can survive temperatures of 36°C for 4 weeks and 39°C for up to 36 hours (Dawes 1987). As much as 90% of the biomass of *T. testudinum* can be in belowground tissue, making this species especially important for its sediment stabilizing abilities (Zieman 1982). *H. wrightii* has narrow leaves and a shallow root and rhizome system. While it is a rapid colonizer, it has less sediment stabilization ability than *T. testudinum* and *S. filiforme*. While all of these seagrasses are important, *T. testudinum* has the highest total habitat values and services (Zieman 1982).

Seagrass beds in high current and/or wave areas typically develop along channel bands and shoals in the form of discrete, mounded patches. In quiescent areas, seagrasses form a more continuous cover, resembling what one generally conceives of as a meadow. The exception to this is when there is insufficient unconsolidated sediment on top of underlying bedrock for the plants to root. In these instances, even though the area may be a quiet backwater, seagrasses will only be able to grow in depressions in the bedrock where sufficient sediments exist (Fonseca 1990).

Main factors influencing seagrass distribution in shallow coastal waters include nutrient availability, light, temperature, and salinity (Tomasko and Lapointe 1991; Fourqurean et al. 1992b). Studies have shown that *T. testudinum*, the dominant seagrass in the FKNMS, is limited primarily by phosphorus (Powell et al. 1989; Fourqurean et al. 1992a). The availability of phosphorus, principally in subsurface sediment waters, limits development of grass beds and controls their composition (Fourqurean et al. 1995).

Fonseca (1990) gives an extensive listing of the characteristics and functions performed by seagrasses as follows:

1) a high rate of leaf growth,
2) the support of large numbers of epiphytic organisms (which are grazed extensively by herbivores),
3) the rapid leaf production results in large quantities of organic material that decomposes in the meadow or is transported to adjacent systems. Since few organisms graze directly on the living seagrasses, the detritus formed from leaves supports a complex food web,
4) shoots retard or slow currents, thereby enhancing sediment stability and increasing the accumulation of organic and inorganic material,
5) roots bind sediments, reducing erosion and preserving sediment microflora,
6) plant and detritus production influence nutrient cycling between sediments and overlying waters,
7) decomposition of rhizomes provides a significant and long-term source of nutrients for sediment microheterotrophs (microscopic organisms unable to synthesize their own food),
8) roots and leaves provide horizontal and vertical complexity which, coupled with abundant and varied food resources, leads to densities of fauna generally exceeding those in unvegetated habitats, and
9) movement of water and fauna transports living and dead organic matter (particulate and dissolved) out of seagrass systems to adjacent habitats.

3.9.2 Benthic Organisms

Seagrass habitats are extremely important for the productivity of fisheries and wildlife in south Florida. Extensive submarine seagrass meadows bridge the distances between coral reefs and mangroves, which have vastly different physical requirements. Early studies emphasized the role of mangrove habitats as a food source and nursery. The results of more recent investigations suggest that seagrass beds in open water environments and within mangrove-lined bays contain the densest populations of organisms. Studies in south Florida bays show that a large proportion of the annual landings depend on seagrass habitat, and there is a clear association between fisheries catch and seagrass cover (Zieman et al. 1989).

A number of invertebrate groups depend on seagrass habitat, including arthropodans, echinoderms, mollusks (almost 200 species), annelids and porifera. The structure of the grass carpet with its calm water and shaded microhabitats provides living space for a rich epifauna of both mobile and sessile organisms. It is these organisms that are of greatest importance to higher consumers within the grass beds, especially fish (Zieman 1982).

Another important feature on many shallow banks is the inconspicuous populations of *Porites furcata* and *Porites porites*. Living and dead colonies of *Porites furcata* provide habitat for many species of invertebrates, including brittle stars, shrimp, crabs, anemones, and young spiny lobster, *Panulirus argus*. Various species of juvenile tropical fish also find shelter and food in and around the intertwining branches of this diminutive but prolific coral (Hudson 1993).

3.9.3 Fish and Invertebrate Populations

Many marine groups or species of fishes found within the FKNMS hold recreational and commercial value (NOAA 1995a; Acosta et al. 1998). Some of the most important recreational fishes are gray snapper, spotted sea trout, red drum and snook (Schmidt and Alvarado 1998). Four invertebrate species found in the FKNMS have important recreational and commercial value to the South Florida economy: blue crab, stone crab, spiny lobster and pink shrimp. Tropical seagrass meadows can support a high diversity of fish species. For example, in a large-scale sampling study in Florida Bay, 92 species of fish comprising 42 families were collected (Thayer et al. 1987). A listing of the families found in the survey is presented in Table 3-3. Densities of fishes are typically greater in seagrass habitat within south Florida's estuaries and coastal lagoons than in adjacent habitats. However, recent work has demonstrated that mean densities of certain macrofaunal communities (fishes and decapods) are usually significantly higher in *T. testudinum* beds than in *H. wrightii* or other surrounding habitats, although the reverse was true for species richness and diversity (Sheridan et at. 1997).

20

Table 3-3. Families of fishes collected by bottom and surface trawling in Everglades National Park (Florida Bay) during 1984 and 1985.

Family Name	Common Name	Family Name	Common Name
Albulidae	Bonefishes	Antennariidae	Frogfishes
Ariidae	Sea catfishes	Atherinidae	Sliversides
Balistidae	Leatherjackets	Batrachoididae	Toadfishes
Belonidae	Needlefishes	Blenniidae	Blennies
Bothidae	Flounder	Bythitidae	Brotulas
Callionymidae	Dragonets	Carangidae	Jacks
Clinidae	Clinids	Clupidae	Herrings
Cynoglossidae	Tonguefishes	Cyprinodontidae	Killifishes
Dasyatidae	Stingrays	Diodontidae	Porcupinefish
Echeneidae	Remoras	Engraulidae	Anchovies
Ephippidae	Spadefishes	Exocoetidae	Flyingfishes
Gerreidae	Mojarras	Gobiesocidae	Clingfishes
Gobiidae	Gobies	Haemulidae	Grunts
Lutjanidae	Snappers	Mugilidae	Mullets
Ogcocephalidae	Batfishes	Ostraciidae	Boxfishes
Poeciliidae	Livebearers	Scaridae	Parrotfishes
Sciaenidae	Drums	Serranidae	Sea Basses
Soleidae	Soles	Sparidae	Porgies
Sphyraenidae	Barracudas	Sphyrnidae	Sharks
Syngnathidae	Pipfishes	Synodontidae	Lizardfishes
Tetraodontidae	Puffers	Triglidae	Searobins

Source: adapted from Thayer et al. 1987

3.9.4 Endangered and Threatened Species

Several species of turtles and marine mammals that frequent seagrass banks in the FKNMS are listed as federal or state endangered or threatened species. Federally endangered species of sea turtles in the FKNMS include the leatherback turtle (*Dermochelys coriacea*), green turtle (*Chelonia mydas*), Kemp's ridley turtle (*Lepidochelys kempii*), and hawksbill turtle (*Eretmochelys imbricata*). In addition, the loggerhead turtle (*Caretta caretta*), listed federally as threatened, also frequents the waters of the Florida Keys. In Florida, marine turtles are provided protection through Florida's Marine Turtle Protection Act and the federal Endangered Species Act (ESA) of 1973, as amended (16 U.S.C. §§ 1531 et seq.).

An endangered marine mammal that might occur in the area is the West Indian manatee (*Trichechus manatus*), a species indigenous to the Florida Keys. Another common mammalian visitor is the bottle nosed dolphin (*Tursiops truncatus*). Marine mammals are protected under the Marine Mammals Protection Act of 1972 (16 U.S.C. §1361 et seq.), and some are also protected by the ESA of 1973.

As adults, the federally listed species of turtles are not year-round residents of seagrass banks in the FKNMS, but are known to occur in or travel through the area during seasonal migrations (see Table 3-4). The annual sea turtle nesting and hatching season in Monroe County, Florida is considered to be April 15 to October 31. Although adult turtles might feed while in the vicinity of shallow banks, they have no specific dependence on them. Because they are an important nesting area for several turtle species, the Florida Keys maintain year-round populations of juvenile turtles. Prior to beginning their seasonal migrations, juvenile turtles rely on extensive seagrass beds for foraging. With the exception of manatees, marine mammals do not depend on the seagrass banks for food, shelter, or necessary mating habitat (Lott 1996). In Monroe County, manatees range from upper Key Largo to Key West and generally inhabit

21

canals, creeks, and surrounding waters throughout the year. A variety of birds feed or nest near seagrass banks, and perch on bird stakes in the area.

Table 3-4. Endangered and threatened species occurring in seagrass habitats within the FKNMS

Species	Approximate Time of Occurrence	Listing Government and Status
Leatherback turtle	April to July*	Federal & State- Endangered
Green sea turtle	June to September*	Federal & State- Endangered
Kemp's ridley turtle	April to June*	Federal & State- Endangered
Hawksbill turtle	July to October*	Federal & State- Endangered
Loggerhead turtle	April to June*	Federal & State- Threatened
West Indian manatee	Varies	Federal & State- Endangered
Arctic peregrine falcon	Fall and winter	State- Endangered
Florida sandhill crane	Varies	State- Threatened
Least tern	Varies	Federal- Endangered; State- Threatened
Roseate tern	Varies	Federal & State- Threatened
Piping plover	Varies	Federal & State- Threatened
Southeastern snowy plover	Varies	State- Threatened

* Juvenile turtles inhabit the Florida Keys year-round. Adults are seasonal migrants.

Source: FFWCC 2004, USFWS 2004

3.10 CULTURAL RESOURCES

3.10.1 Background

European contact in the Florida Keys began with Spanish explorers in the 1500s. Spanish control of the Florida Keys region lasted into the 1700s. During this period, the Spanish established a chain of missionaries across what is now the State of Florida and also established a small but prosperous maritime trade network based in Cuba. The number of ships increased in the Florida Keys as other European countries began to travel to their colonies in the Americas. The shipping industry experienced a dramatic increase in volume during the period of 1700 to 1820 as trade and maritime technology made great advances. Also during that time, wreckers began to salvage cargoes from ships that had run aground on the Florida reef tract.

From 1820 to 1865, coastal commerce continued to grow, and coastal forts were constructed to defend the nation's southern boundary, particularly during the Civil War. This time period was also marked by the Seminole wars. The Seminoles were the predominant Native American group in the area before complete Euro-American settlement, with the Tequesta and Calusa pre-dating the Seminoles. From 1865 to 1912, various coastal ports began to flourish in Florida, a system of lighthouses was developed to aid in coastal navigation, and the American Merchant Marines and the modern Navy were established (Terrell 1994). Because the Florida Keys are located on important trade routes, shipwrecks have occurred in the area for centuries. Historically, Spanish ships dominated the waters in the Keys. Hurricanes, reefs, and military conflicts claimed hundreds of Spanish ships; in some cases, entire fleets were lost in the area (Terrell 1994). Salvage operations for shipwrecks began as early as the mid-1500s. Various groups (e.g., Spaniards, French, Dutch, English, Calusa Indians) are documented to have attempted recovery of vessels lost in the Keys (Terrell 1994).

3.10.2 Potential Historic Resources in Grounding Areas Within the FKNMS

Pre-Historic Remains - Lower sea levels during the Pleistocene ice ages made parts of the Continental Shelf accessible to primitive human groups then populating the Americas via the Bering Land Bridge

(10,000 to 12,000 years before present). A Minerals Management Service (MMS) report on the region cites a poor probability for locating prehistoric remains at lower depths due to later human habitation after the area was inundated. Also, the apparent sea level rise in the area was slow, allowing for destruction of site remains by natural wave action and environmental forces. MMS considers the Florida Keys to have little potential for submerged prehistoric sites (Continental Shelf Associates, Inc. 1990).

Native American Remains – Today, it is impossible to predict which seagrass banks and environs constituted a habitable island during the late prehistoric to European contact stages. It is possible that these islands were inhabited or visited by the maritime Calusa Indian people. There is a slightly better chance of Native American cultural remains in areas associated with the Calusa between 2500 years before present to European contact.

Historic Period Remains - Between the Spanish regional presence in the sixteenth century through the late nineteenth century, the region was sparsely populated. However, shipwreck remains do exist in the Keys, primarily of Spanish, Portuguese, British, and U.S. origin (Terrell 1994). NOAA and designated contractors will follow state and federal guidelines to ensure that restoration actions at injury sites do not in any way adversely impact historical remains, if present, to the extent that if deemed necessary, restoration may not occur or be significantly modified.

The coordinates of injury sites will be overlaid on a map of archeological/cultural resource site boundaries, provided by the Florida Division of Historic Resources, to determine if there is any overlap. The map includes archaeological sites for Monroe County, FL (including archaeological site boundaries and basic site attributes as recorded in the Florida Master Site File), field survey areas (containing cultural resource field survey project boundaries and basic survey attributes as recorded in the Florida Master Site File), and the National Register of Historic Places within the State of Florida. If there is no overlap, restoration of the injured resource will proceed as laid out in this document, unless what may be an archeological or cultural resource is found at the site during the assessment process. In this case, or in the case that the injured site does overlap with the archeological/cultural resource site boundaries, a survey of the area will be undertaken by an archeologist to determine whether or not restoration should be undertaken. One hundred eighty seven injury sites have already been overlaid, the representations of which can be found below (Figures 3-3 and 3-4).

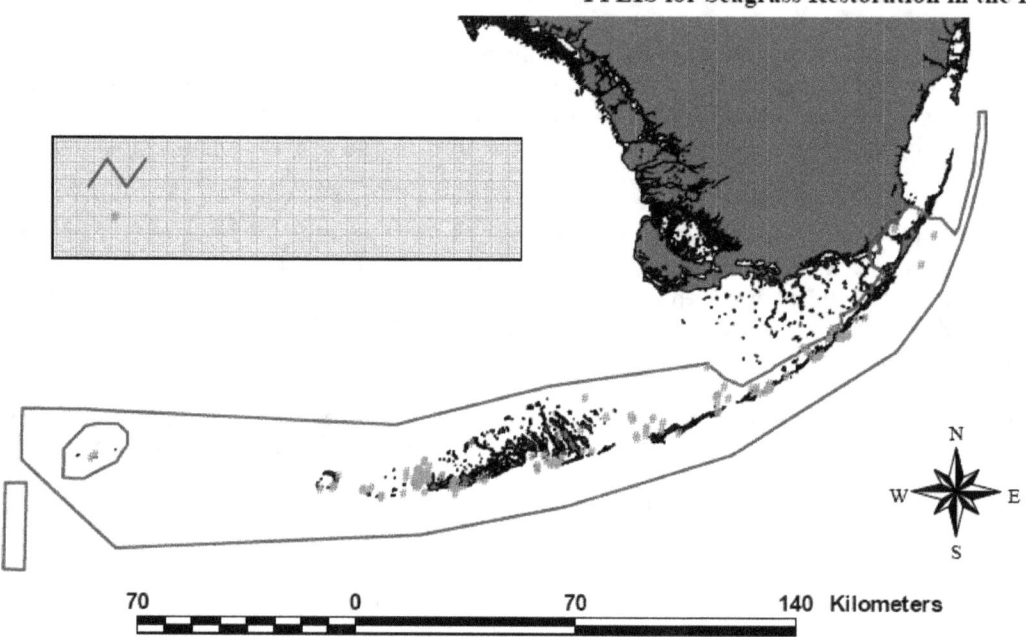

70   0   70   140 Kilometers

Figure 3-3. Location of 187 seagrass grounding cases that were assessed between
October 2000 and July 2004.

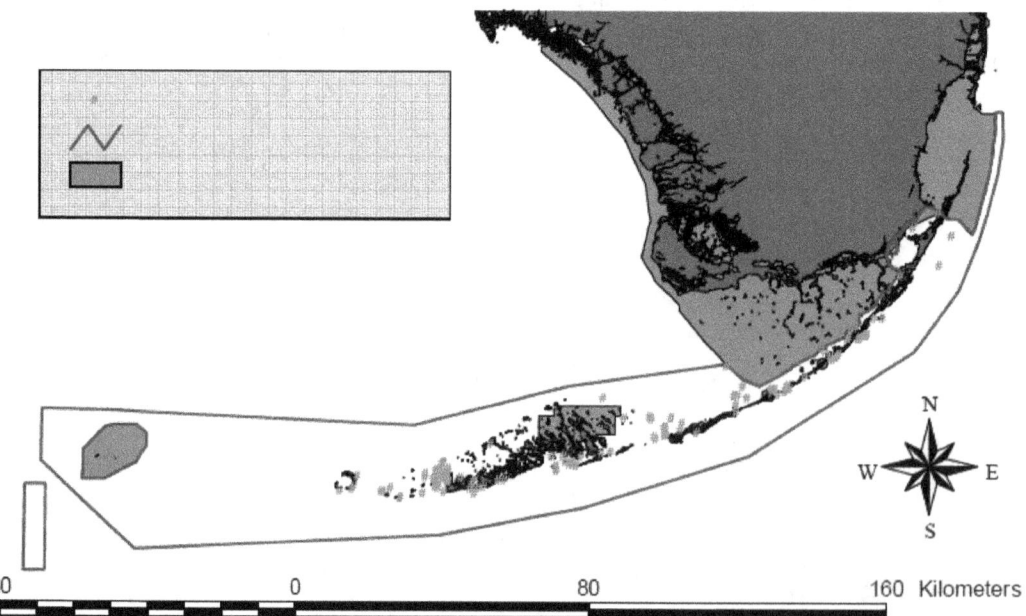

80   0   80   160 Kilometers

Figure 3-4. Seagrass groundings in relation to the field surveys as recorded at the Florida
Master Site File. Five seagrass cases within the FKNMS are inside field surveys.

3.11 HAZARDOUS AND TOXIC SUBSTANCES

Hazardous and toxic substances typically include (1) materials currently used as part of day-to-day manufacturing operations, (2) regulated substances such as asbestos and lead-based paints, and (3) any improperly disposed-of materials such as spilled or buried hazardous waste. None of these materials are expected to be encountered at the restoration sites due to their relatively remote locations. There are no Superfund sites located in Monroe County, Florida. The United States Environmental Protection Agency's (USEPA) database indicates only one nearby Emergency Planning and Community Right-to-Know Act (EPCRA) Toxic Release Site in Marathon, FL: the Royal Palm Ice Plant, from which there has not been a reported release since 1988 (USEPA 1999b).

3.12 SOCIOECONOMICS

3.12.1 Region of Influence

The socioeconomic indicators described in this section include regional economic activity, employment statistics, and demographics. These indicators characterize the region of influence (ROI). An ROI is a geographic area selected as a basis on which the social and economic impacts of projects are analyzed. The ROI is the area most affected by changes resulting from project implementation and is usually based on where project employees reside, local commuting and purchasing patterns, and the size and scope of the proposed project. Typically, a county is the smallest unit of analysis for an ROI. Because seagrass restoration is relatively limited in scope and will involve few workers over a short period, the ROI for the social and economic environment is defined as Monroe County, Florida. Although residents of nearby counties, such as Broward and Dade, may be indirectly affected by project implementation (i.e. they may vacation in the Keys and fish on the seagrass banks or have insurance companies that also cover residents in the Florida Keys) they will not be directly affected. Additionally, the economic base of these nearby counties is much more highly diversified into areas other than fishing and tourism than that of Monroe County.

Because a high percentage of Monroe County residents often use the banks for recreational and commercial fishing and conduct commercial tourism activities (approximately 46%) (English et. al. 1996), they will directly benefit from the restoration of seagrass banks to their baseline conditions. Additionally, the protection from storm events that seagrass banks provide has an impact on the vulnerability and value of their homes. However, because the dollar value of the restoration actions themselves is low, they will not create a significant number of jobs for Monroe county residents.

3.12.2 Regional Economic Activity

The primary sources of employment in the ROI are services, retail trade, and government services. As shown in Table 3-5, these sectors accounted for more than 75 percent of the county's total employment in 1999. The economy of Monroe County is heavily dependent on tourism. In 1996, proprietor's employment accounted for more than 21 percent of the county's total employment, compared to 14.5 percent for Florida and 16.4 percent for the United States (USDOC 1998). This statistic indicates the central importance of small businesses in the tourist economy. A recent study estimated that tourist/recreational activities provided more than 46 percent of the county's employment and about 60 percent of the county's total economic output (English et al. 1996). Consistent with these statistics, four of the six largest employers in the county are tourism related.

25

Table 3-5. ROI Employment by Major Sectors (2000 Monroe County)

Employment Sector	Percent of Total Employment
Services	39.4
Retail Trade	29.7
Government	8.8
Construction	6.2
Transportation, Com, Utilities	6.8
Finance, Insurance, Real Estate	4.8
Wholesale Trade	2.3
Manufacturing	1.6
Agricultural, Forest, Fisheries	0.9

Source: Key West Chamber of Commerce 2002

In 1997 to 1998, recreating visitors to the Florida Keys spent an estimated $1.38 billion in Monroe County (Leeworthy and Vanasse 1999). In addition, a significant number of retired persons live in Monroe County, generating a large amount of income in transfer payments flowing into the local economy in the form of pensions, retirement pay, dividends and interest on investments, and social security. In 2000, an estimated 15 percent of the total population was 65 years of age or older. This creates a base of income in Monroe County that is independent of employment. In 1999, the per capita income was $34,456, which is higher than the overall Florida per capita income average of $27,781 (Key West Chamber of Commerce 2002).

The military and commercial fishing industry are also important sectors of the region's economy. The unemployment rate for Monroe County was 2.5 percent in 2001, compared to 5.2 percent for the United States (Florida Keys Chamber of Commerce 2002). It should be noted that much of the employment is seasonal and rates vary during the year.

3.12.3 Demographics

In 2000, the population of Monroe County was estimated to be 79,589. In comparison to the previous decade where the population increased by 23.5% (1980-1990), the population of Monroe Country increased by only 2% from 1990 to 2000. The population is projected to continue to grow, though at a slower rate. The population is projected to reach more than 101,000 by 2010, a 1.5 percent growth rate. Table 3-6 shows the racial/ethnic breakdown of the population estimates for 2000.

Table 3-6. Demographics of Monroe County

Race / Ethnicity	Percent of Total Population (1997)
White not Hispanic	77.2
Black not Hispanic	4.5
Hispanic	15.8
Other	2.5

Source: Key West Chamber of Commerce 2002

Peak tourist populations occur from January to March of each year. The tourist season is longer in the Upper Keys than in the Lower Keys, extending from January to August, and is based on weekend tourists from Miami and south Florida. The functional population (the sum of the peak seasonal and resident population) was 159,113 in 2000 (Monroe County Growth Management 2001). The seasonal population accounts for nearly 56 percent of the functional population during the peak tourist season.

3.13 QUALITY OF LIFE

Within the FKNMS are nationally significant marine environments, including seagrass meadows, mangrove islands, and extensive living coral reefs (NOAA 1996b). The quality of life of many residents in the Keys depends on the condition of these marine ecosystems. A survey of Monroe County residents regarding their recreational activities conducted by NOAA's Strategic Environmental Assessments Division (1997), found that 77 percent of residents participated in some form of outdoor recreation in the Keys. Thirty-two percent rated the quality of life in Monroe County as "excellent", while over 46% rated it as "good". Less than five percent rated it as "poor". Those who participated in outdoor recreation activities gave higher quality of life ratings than those that did not. Factors hypothesized to be related to outdoor recreation participation (e.g. climate, water activities, environment and access to natural resources) were among the top ten most important reasons for living in Monroe County. Those that participated in outdoor recreation activities rated these reasons higher than those that did not (NOAA 1995a; NOAA 1996b).

CHAPTER 4. ENVIRONMENTAL AND SOCIOECONOMIC CONSEQUENCES

4.1 INTRODUCTION

This section describes the potential environmental and socioeconomic consequences of the restoration alternatives presented in this document. The restoration alternatives to be discussed include: 1) no action, 2) seagrass transplants, 3) bird stakes 4) fertilizer spikes, 5) sediment fill, 6) sediment tubes, 7) berm redistribution, 8) sod replacement, 9) water markers, and 10) exclusion cages. The direct and indirect effects of each alternative are discussed with respect to 13 resource categories. For five of these categories, both the direct and indirect effects are identical for all 10 restoration actions. These categories are discussed in this introduction, and are not repeated in the individual restoration alternative sections. The effects (adverse and/or beneficial), or lack thereof, are described according to duration (short-term or long-term) and intensity (minor or major). As this document is not action-specific, the potential impacts are discussed in general terms for a restoration site that may include the combination of propeller scars, blowholes, and berms. For restoration cases that present the possibility for unique or controversial environmental or socioeconomic impacts, additional project-specific analyses will be necessary.

4.1.1 Surrounding Land Use (All Restoration Alternatives)

Direct Effects: No direct effects are expected.

Indirect Effects: No indirect effects are expected.

4.1.2 Climate (All Restoration Alternatives)

Direct Effects: No direct effects are expected.

Indirect Effects: No indirect effects are expected.

4.1.3 Air Quality (All Restoration Alternatives)

Direct Effects: Short-term minor adverse effects are expected related to the use of motorized vessels to complete the restoration actions. Given the relatively short period of the restoration actions, the total emission amounts will create negligible impacts to local and regional air quality.

Indirect Effects: No indirect effects are expected.

4.1.4 Noise (All Restoration Alternatives)

Direct Effects: Short-term minor adverse effects are expected from motorized vessel traffic to the restoration site. Given the short time period of restoration implementation, negligible effects are anticipated.

Indirect Effects: No indirect effects are expected.

4.1.5 Cultural Resources (All Restoration Alternatives)

Direct Effects: Short and long-term adverse direct effects are possible if the disturbance of the sediment by the restoration actions advances deterioration of cultural resources. Restoration contractors under the supervision of NOAA and/or State personnel will be instructed to halt all activities if cultural resources are discovered until authorization to continue is granted by State and Federal cultural resource authorities, including the State Historic Preservation Officer.

Indirect Effects: No indirect effects are expected.

4.2 NO ACTION ALTERNATIVE

Under this alternative, no action would be taken at the grounding site, relying exclusively on the processes of natural recovery.

Pros: Since this option is non-intrusive, the existing regrowth, if present, will be left intact. This includes all the algae and seagrass growth that may have occurred since the time of the injury. In addition, the potential for further groundings associated with restoration equipment and vessels is avoided. The potential for adverse effects from sediment dispersion and turbidity in the adjacent intact seagrass areas are also avoided.

Cons: The no action alternative may result in natural recovery on a longer time scale or it may lead to further deterioration of the bank system. Without restoration, grounding scars may remain as a morphological feature distinct from the surrounding environment over a long time period. The potential instability of the site may also contribute to further sediment migration, decline in primary production, erosion, and impact to adjacent seagrass banks. In addition, natural revegetation could also allow the colonization and establishment of undesirable, opportunistic (such as blue-green algae) or invasive species, rather than the desired species of seagrass.

4.2.1 Location and Area Use (No Action Alternative)

Direct Effects: No direct effects are expected unless natural recovery fails to take place, in which case further deterioration of the area may occur, leaving surrounding areas vulnerable to erosion and decreasing the habitat and food source for a variety of organisms.

Indirect Effects: Long-term minor adverse effects are expected. Without restoration, the quality of the marine habitat in the FKNMS will be, in part, diminished, resulting in a possible reduction in commercial and recreational industries directly and indirectly dependent on a healthy marine ecosystem. Additionally, in many instances, without restoration, the grounding area has a higher probability of further degradation from severe storms.

4.2.2 Geology (No Action Alternative)

Direct Effects: Short and long-term adverse effects on adjacent undamaged habitats may occur as the original injury location may expand due to water current and storm related erosion.

Indirect Effects: No indirect effects are expected.

4.2.3 Water Resources (No Action Alternative)

Direct Effects: Long-term minor adverse effects are expected. Higher-than-normal turbidity levels may result from modified current flows, sediment dispersal, the absence of a secure seagrass root and rhizome system, and annual storm events.

Indirect Effects: Marine resources, such as coral reefs, dependent on the high water clarity and quality sustained by healthy seagrass communities may suffer.

4.2.4 Biological Resources (No Action Alternative)

Direct Effects: Long-term minor adverse effects are expected depending on the scale and severity of the injury. In a high-energy environment or after severe storm events, regrowth may be initiated and destroyed many times before stable colonization is established.

The federally listed species of turtles are likely not to be permanent residents of the injured seagrass banks as adults, but rather are known to occur in or travel through the area during seasonal migrations. Although they may feed while in the vicinity of the injured bank, they have no specific dependence on it. Because these species merely pass through the area and are not anticipated to depend exclusively on the injured seagrass bank for food or habitat, the adoption of the no action alternative is not expected to result in adverse effects on them, other than loss of a small segment of potential feeding area. However, juvenile marine turtles are year-round residents of the Florida Keys and rely heavily on seagrass beds for foraging. As it is expected that the no action alternative will result in a longer time to recovery or injury expansion, it is expected that there would be long-term minor adverse effects on juvenile turtles from this alternative.

For fauna that is seagrass dependent for all or part of their life cycles, several direct adverse effects are expected. These include a partial loss of a food source and loss of substratum for epiphyte production for the numerous epiphytic grazing species. Also, cryptic fauna that use seagrass blades for cover, especially during their juvenile phase, will be, in part, adversely affected.

Indirect Effects: Long-term adverse indirect effects on the seagrass community are expected until the site has reached a recovery level similar to baseline conditions. The loss of habitat for seagrass-dwelling species will result in a reduction in the abundance and diversity of other species sheltering or feeding in the seagrass. The abundance of predatory fish that feed on seagrass-dependent organisms will be adversely impacted by the lost seagrass habitat. In addition, the expansion of berm sediment dispersal is expected during storms, thereby encroaching on and possibly damaging nearby communities.

Depending on the size of the injury, long-term adverse impacts are expected as a result of increased turbidity. Light levels may be decreased, which will affect surrounding photosynthetic biota such as corals, benthic algae, and phytoplankton. Additionally, increased turbidity levels may affect zooplankton by excluding them from areas of high turbidity.

Endangered and threatened species would likely experience no indirect effects.

4.2.5 Infrastructure (No Action Alternative)

Direct Effects: No direct effects are expected.

Indirect Effects: No indirect effects are expected.

4.2.6 Hazardous and Toxic Substances (No Action Alternative)

Direct Effects: No direct effects are expected.

Indirect Effects: No indirect effects are expected.

4.2.7 Socioeconomics (No Action Alternative)

Direct Effects: No major direct effects are expected.

Indirect Effects: Long-term minor adverse effects are expected as a result of the cumulative impact of seagrass habitat degradation. It is expected that over time, continued habitat degradation will impact the recreational and commercial tourism and fishing industries.

4.2.8 Quality of Life (No Action Alternative)

Direct Effects: Viewing injured seagrass beds is expected to slightly diminish the quality of the recreational experience enjoyed by residents and tourists.

Indirect Effects: Long-term minor adverse effects are expected as the cumulative impact of seagrass injuries will impact the viability of recreational and commercial activities dependent on healthy seagrass ecosystems.

4.3 SEAGRASS TRANSPLANT ALTERNATIVE

Under this alternative, seagrass colonizing stems are directly transplanted into the injured area to stabilize the sediment. Collection methods have been developed which minimize impact to donor beds of *H. wrightii* and *S. filiforme* and assure rapid recovery after plants have been removed (Fonseca et al. 1998). There is no evidence that any invasive or exotic species have occupied donor sites. This restoration technique helps advance the injury recovery process and the associated direct and indirect ecological and socioeconomic benefits.

Pros: Seagrass transplants are complementary to any site regrowth of seagrasses or algae. The potential for adverse effects from sediment dispersion and turbidity to the adjacent intact seagrass areas is also reduced as the seagrass transplants will facilitate substrate stability and expedited site recovery.

Cons: If not carefully monitored, collection of transplant source stock may degrade donor sites. To prevent this possibility, state and/or NOAA seagrass biologists will routinely monitor the impact of transplant source stock collection on donor sites.

4.3.1 Location and Area Use (Seagrass Transplants)

Direct Effects: No direct effects are expected.

Indirect Effects: Long-term minor beneficial indirect effects are expected. The transplanting of seagrass will facilitate conditions amenable for seagrass recruitment and the return of associated flora and fauna. This, in turn, is expected to support, in part, recreational and/or commercial activities that depend to some degree on healthy seagrass ecosystems.

4.3.2 Geology (Seagrass Transplants)

Direct Effects: Positive short and long-term direct impacts are anticipated, as seagrass transplants will help stabilize sediment in the injured area, thereby reducing the chance for additional site erosion.

Indirect Effects: No indirect effects are expected.

4.3.3 Water Resources (Seagrass Transplants)

Direct Effects: Short and long term beneficial direct effects are expected as seagrass transplants and subsequent healthy seagrass recovery over the injured area will reduce water turbidity.

Indirect Effects: Beneficial long term indirect effects are expected as decreased water turbidity provides clearer water, an environmental amenity that is enjoyed by visitors and residents of the Florida Keys.

4.3.4 Biological Resources (Seagrass Transplants)

Direct Effects: Short and long term beneficial direct effects are anticipated as seagrass transplants will facilitate a more rapid recovery of the injury site, thereby improving habitat for seagrass dependent flora and fauna. The food provision and nursery protection services the injured area provided to fish prior to injury will be more quickly restored. Additionally, seagreass transplants will permit the faster redevelopment of epiphytic and algal communities in the injured area. Endangered and threatened species would likely experience no direct effects.

Indirect Effects: Beneficial long-term benefits are anticipated as a recovery of the injured site represents, in part, an improvement in the overall health of the seagrass ecosystem and numerous biological resources that indirectly benefit. By decreasing turbidity, the restored seagrass indirectly benefits both autotrophic and heterotrophic benthic organisms in nearby communities, including those found on associated coral reefs. Endangered and threatened species would likely experience no indirect effects.

4.3.5 Infrastructure (Seagrass Transplants)

Direct Effects: Short-term minor adverse effects are expected as restoration activities will generate small increases in solid waste (refuse).

Indirect Effects: No indirect effects are expected.

4.3.6 Hazardous and Toxic Substances (Seagrass Transplants)

Direct Effects: No direct effects are expected.

Indirect Effects: No indirect effects are expected.

4.3.7 Socioeconomics (Seagrass Transplants)

Direct Effects: No direct effects are expected.

Indirect Effects: Long-term beneficial indirect effects are anticipated as seagrass transplants will contribute toward overall recovery of the injured area and contribute, in part, toward the viability of recreational and commercial activities directly and indirectly dependent on healthy seagrass ecosystems.

4.3.8 Quality of Life (Seagrass Transplants)

Direct Effects: No direct effects are expected.

Indirect Effects: Long-term beneficial indirect effects are anticipated as successful restoration of the injured area will contribute, in part, toward an overall healthy seagrass ecosystem. This, in turn, helps support the viability of commercial and recreational activities that are directly or indirectly dependent on seagrass ecosystems.

4.4 BIRD STAKE ALTERNATIVE

This alternative involves the placement of polyvinyl chloride (PVC) bird roosting stakes in portions of the injured area. Bird stakes provide a platform for birds to roost, and, as a result, feces are deposited into the waters directly above the injury area, thereby fertilizing the re-colonizing seagrasses.

Pros: This alternative directly addresses the potential instability of the injured areas by facilitating a more rapid regrowth of seagrasses. During the time that bird stakes are present, they may serve as restoration site markers, thereby reducing the potential for additional accidental groundings. In addition, it is anticipated that with enough public education, passing boaters will recognize the bird stakes as an indication of an active restoration project, and by association, exercise greater caution when navigating in the area and in other shallow waters.

Cons: Depending on the location of the grounding site and the quantity of bird stakes required, aesthetic concerns may be an issue. The possibility for vandalism and additional groundings in the immediate area due to boats mistaking the bird stakes as water markers exist. The possibility also exists for navigational incidents with the bird stakes, however, this possibility is low as stakes are placed only in shallow water, typically removed from the primary channels. To address these concerns, the FKNMS and FDEP are continually engaged with the local community on seagrass restoration education programs. Additionally, research has demonstrated that, if left on site too long, bird stakes may cause a communal shift of seagrass species from *T. testudinum* to *H. wrightii* (Powell et al. 1989). Thus, bird stakes are removed after approximately 75% survival coalescence is reached, usually after 18 months.

4.4.1 Location and Area Uses (Bird Stakes)

Direct Effects: Depending on the length of time that bird stakes are required at the site, the areas immediately below and adjacent to the bird stakes are likely to be temporarily incompatible for the use of anglers or boaters. In most instances, the impact on boaters will be limited as grounding locations are in shallow waters that should not be regularly visited. The impact for anglers is limited to the duration that the bird stakes are positioned at the site.

Indirect Effects: Long-term minor beneficial indirect effects are expected as bird stakes will facilitate conditions amenable for seagrass recruitment and the return of associated fauna. It would be expected to hasten the return of recreational and/or commercial water based activities to the general area.

4.4.2 Geology (Bird Stakes)

Direct Effects: No adverse direct effects are expected. Long-term beneficial direct effects are anticipated as bird stakes will facilitate stabilization of the sediment in the injury area, thus, reducing the possibility of future site erosion.

Indirect Effects: No indirect effects are expected.

4.4.3 Water Resources (Bird Stakes)

Direct Effects: No direct effects on water quality or on the biological resources within the substrate that depend on high water quality have been detected in experiments or are anticipated in restoration actions.

Indirect Effects: No indirect effects are expected.

4.4.4 Biological Resources (Bird Stakes)

Direct Effects: Short and long term beneficial direct effects are anticipated for the seagrass communities. However, if left on site too long, bird stakes may cause a communal shift of seagrass species from *T. testudinum* to *H. wrightii* (Powell 1989). The food provision and nursery protection services the injured area provided to fish prior to injury will be more quickly restored. Additionally, seagreass transplants will permit the faster redevelopment of epiphytic and algal communities in the injured area. Endangered and threatened species would likely experience no direct effects.

33

<u>Indirect Effects:</u> Short and long term beneficial indirect effects are anticipated as the recovery of the site will benefit seagrass dependent flora and fauna. By decreasing turbidity, the restored seagrass indirectly benefits both autotrophic and heterotrophic benthic organisms in nearby communities, including those found on associated coral reefs. Endangered and threatened species would likely experience no indirect effects.

4.4.5 Infrastructure (Bird Stakes)

<u>Direct Effects:</u> Short-term minor adverse effects are expected as restoration activities will generate small increases in solid waste (refuse).

<u>Indirect Effects:</u> No indirect effects are expected.

4.4.6 Hazardous and Toxic Substances (Bird Stakes)

<u>Direct Effects:</u> No direct effects are expected.

<u>Indirect Effects:</u> No indirect effects are expected.

4.4.7 Socioeconomics (Bird Stakes)

<u>Direct Effects:</u> No direct effects are expected.

<u>Indirect Effects:</u> Long-term beneficial indirect effects are anticipated as bird stakes will contribute toward overall recovery of the injured area and as such contribute, in part, toward the viability of recreational and commercial activities dependent on healthy seagrass ecosystems.

4.4.8 Quality of Life (Bird Stakes)

<u>Direct Effects:</u> Depending on the location of the restoration site and the scale of the project, the stakes may be viewed by some as an adverse aesthetic concern. For others, the stakes may improve quality of life as residents and visitors will take interest and satisfaction in seeing on-going seagrass restoration projects.

<u>Indirect Effects:</u> Long-term beneficial indirect effects are anticipated as successful restoration of the injured area will contribute, in part, toward an overall healthy seagrass ecosystem. This, in turn, helps support the viability of commercial and recreational activities that are directly or indirectly dependent on seagrass ecosystems.

4.5 FERTILIZER SPIKE ALTERNATIVE

This alternative involves the placement of chemical fertilizer spikes (e.g. tree spikes) in portions of the injury to enhance recovery of transplanted or naturally re-colonizing seagrasses. One fertilizer spike will be placed next to each seagrass transplant. Nitrogen, phosphorous, and potassium comprise the main chemical makeup of these spikes, which studies have not shown to negatively affect the surrounding area (Williams 1990).

Pros: This alternative directly addresses the potential instability of the injured area by facilitating a more rapid regrowth of seagrasses, both transplanted and from colonizing seagrasses. Fertilizer spikes provide a means to enhance the fertilization of an injured area when water depths are too great for bird stakes. Fertilizer is released steadily over a three to four month period, thereby providing a constant flow of nutrient enrichment. Unlike bird stakes, fertilizer spikes cannot be vandalized or potentially confused as water markers.

Cons: Depending on the site-specific sediment and water current conditions at the grounding site, the efficacy of the fertilizer spikes may be less than three to four months. This may require repeat visits to insert additional fertilizer spikes.

4.5.1 Location and Area Uses (Fertilizer Spikes)

Direct Effects: No direct effects are expected.

Indirect Effects: Long-term minor beneficial indirect effects are expected. The insertion of fertilizer spikes will facilitate conditions amenable for seagrass recruitment and the return of associated flora and fauna. The restoration of this injured area contributes, in part, toward the viability of seagrass dependent recreational and commercial activities in the area.

4.5.2 Geology (Fertilizer Spikes)

Direct Effects: Beneficial effects are anticipated as fertilizer spikes will contribute toward recovery of seagrass in the injured area, and as such, stabilize the sediment, thereby reducing the possibility for additional site erosion.

Indirect Effects: No indirect effects are expected.

4.5.3 Water Resources (Fertilizer Spikes)

Direct Effects: No direct effects are expected.

Indirect Effects: No indirect effects are expected.

4.5.4 Biological Resources (Fertilizer Spikes)

Direct Effects: Long-term direct beneficial effects are anticipated as fertilization of seagrass will expedite recovery of the area and positively impact other seagrass dependent flora and fauna. Additional spikes inserted throughout the year would increase this potential benefit. The food provision and nursery protection services the injured area provided to fish prior to injury will be more quickly restored. Additionally, seagreass transplants will permit the faster redevelopment of epiphytic and algal communities in the injured area. Endangered and threatened species would likely experience no direct effects.

Indirect Effects: By decreasing turbidity, the restored seagrass indirectly benefits both autotrophic and heterotrophic benthic organisms in nearby communities, including those found on associated coral reefs. Endangered and threatened species would likely experience no indirect effects.

4.5.5 Infrastructure (Fertilizer Spikes)

Direct Effects: No direct effects are expected.

Indirect Effects: No indirect effects are expected.

4.5.6 Hazardous and Toxic Substances (Fertilizer Spikes)

Direct Effects: No direct effects are expected as there are no hazardous or toxic substances associated with the chemical fertilizer in the spikes.

Indirect Effects: No indirect effects are expected.

4.5.7 Socioeconomics (Fertilizer Spikes)

Direct Effects: No direct effects are expected

Indirect Effects: Long-term beneficial indirect effects are anticipated as fertilizer spikes will contribute toward overall recovery of the injured area and as such contribute, in part, toward the viability of recreational and commercial activities dependent on healthy seagrass ecosystems.

4.5.8 Quality of Life (Fertilizer Spikes)

Direct Effects: No direct effects are expected.

Indirect Effects: Long-term beneficial indirect effects are anticipated, as successful restoration of the injured area will contribute, in part, toward an overall healthy seagrass ecosystem. This, in turn, helps support the viability of commercial and recreational activities that are directly or indirectly dependent on seagrass ecosystems.

4.6 SEDIMENT FILL ALTERNATIVE

This alternative involves the placement of sediment fill in injury blowholes or deep propeller scars to stabilize the injury, thereby reducing the probability of continued site erosion and providing a suitable substrate for recolonization. In the event that sediment fill is identified as one of the preferred restoration alternatives, the transportation of materials by barge from an upland staging area to the grounding site will be necessary. NOAA and designated contractors will exercise extreme caution to minimize the risk of any additional seagrass injury during the course of restoration activities. This includes the use of temporary moorings and/or sediment turbidity screens while placing sediment fill in blowholes. Restoration contractors will be required to follow current best mooring guidelines as determined by NOAA. U.S. Route 1 is the only major roadway providing access from the south Florida mainland to the Keys. The roadway varies between two and four lanes. Sediment fill and other supplies, if not available locally, will be transported on U.S. Route 1, or brought to the site by barge from another area depending on the final construction plans.

Pros: This alternative directly addresses the potential instability of the injured areas by stabilizing the injury site, thereby facilitating conditions for a more rapid regrowth of seagrasses, and preventing further injury from erosion and other destabilizing forces. Through the filling of blowholes or other injury features, the site can be modified to a state that is more similar to pre-grounding conditions.

Cons: If care is not exercised, the possibility exists for additional grounding injuries from the sediment barge and other vessels used in the restoration process. In addition, for injury sites that have had partial re-colonization, the sediment fill will smother the new growth. However, given that an unrestored blowhole is physically unstable, it is highly likely that any new growth would be dislodged during a major storm event, as it would be exposed to the wind-driven waves from hurricanes (Whitfield 2002).

4.6.1 Location and Area Uses (Sediment Fill)

Direct Effects: Depending on the context of the injury and design of the restoration plan, temporary short-term direct effects may occur in the form of the establishment of no-boating "exclusion zones", marked by buoys, around large restoration sites. However, such an action would only be implemented in the rare case of an exceptionally large seagrass injury and instituted only during the few days in which restoration was taking place.

Indirect Effects: Long-term minor beneficial indirect effects are expected since the placement of fill will at least partially restore the site morphology, and thus make conditions amenable for seagrass recruitment and the return of associated flora and fauna. Recovery of the injury site will assist, in part, the continued viability of recreational and/or commercial activities dependent on healthy seagrass ecosystems.

4.6.2 Geology (Sediment Fill)

Direct Effects: Long-term minor beneficial effects on geology will occur as a result of filling injury features with sediment. A closer approximation to pre-grounding topography will help reestablish the pre-injury baseline conditions at the site.

Short-term minor adverse effects on geology may result from the disturbance of the substrate during filling activities if proper mooring and anchoring of work vessels and equipment is not maintained.

Indirect Effects: No indirect effects are expected.

4.6.3 Water Resources (Sediment Fill)

Direct Effects: Short-term minor adverse effects from increased turbidity generated during placement of sediment fill in the injured areas are expected. However, care will be taken to minimize these effects through the use of the most appropriate and cost effective technology (e.g. turbidity screens). Long-term benefits in improved water quality are expected once seagrass recolonize the injury area.

Indirect Effects: No indirect effects are expected.

4.6.4 Biological Resources (Sediment Fill)

Direct Effects: The placement of sediment fill will provide long-term benefits as the essential substrate for seagrasses that re-colonize the injury area. Re-colonization of the injury area by seagrasses will directly and indirectly benefit numerous species of flora and fauna. The food provision and nursery protection services the injured area provided to fish prior to injury will be more quickly restored. Additionally, seagreass transplants will permit the faster redevelopment of epiphytic and algal communities in the injured area. Endangered and threatened species are not likely to experience direct effects. In the event the seagrass injury is located within an area with known resident populations of manatees, restoration activities will be completed following state manatee protection guidelines ensuring their protection and minimization of overall disturbance.

Indirect Effects: Long-term minor beneficial effects on nearby seagrass and benthic animal communities are expected. The restoration of the injured area with sediment fill will lessen the chances of the surrounding communities being adversely affected by the forces exerted by annual storms, although dispersion of unconsolidated sediment out of the grounding area is still a possibility early in the recovery process.

Fish communities will experience long-term minor beneficial effects. The eventual growth of benthic organisms, including algae, plus an increase in shelter habitat for juvenile fish, will provide additional food sources for fish living on or near the injured area, including the larger predatory species that roam seagrass banks in search of prey. No indirect effects on endangered and threatened species are expected.

4.6.5 Infrastructure (Sediment Fill)

Direct Effects: No direct effects are expected.

Indirect Effects: No indirect effects are expected.

4.6.6 Hazardous and Toxic Substances (Sediment Fill)

Direct Effects: No adverse effects are expected. All efforts will be made to ensure the placement of sediment fill will not introduce significant new hazardous materials into the environment. Most construction materials would come from natural sources (e.g., limestone mined from inland quarries) and be inert. The contractor will be required to address contingencies through plans needed for the permitting process. These contingency plans will include incidental spillage of fuel.

Indirect Effects: No indirect effects are expected.

4.6.7 Socioeconomics (Sediment Fill)

Direct Effects: No direct effects are expected.

Indirect Effects: Long-term minor beneficial effects are expected to occur as sediment fill will improve the likelihood of a successful seagrass restoration project, and in part, an improvement in the seagrass ecology of the area. This, in turn, is positive for recreational and commercial activities that are directly and/or indirectly dependent on a healthy seagrass ecosystem.

4.6.8 Quality of Life (Sediment Fill)

Direct Effects: No direct effects are expected.

Indirect Effects: Long-term beneficial indirect effects are anticipated as successful restoration of the injured area will contribute, in part, toward an overall healthy seagrass ecosystem. This in turn helps support the viability of commercial and recreational activities that are directly or indirectly dependent on seagrass ecosystems.

4.7 SEDIMENT TUBE ALTERNATIVE

This alternative involves the placement of biodegradable fabric mesh tubes filled with sediment, referred hereinafter as "sediment tubes", in propeller scars or other injury features. The placement of sediment tubes helps stabilize the injury location, reduce the probability of continued site erosion, and enhance conditions for seagrass recovery. This restoration technique helps advance the injury recovery process, and by default, the associated direct and indirect ecological and socioeconomic benefits of a healthy seagrass ecosystem.

Pros: This alternative directly addresses restoration of the injured area by stabilizing the injury site, thereby facilitating a more rapid regrowth of transplanted or naturally re-colonizing seagrasses.

Cons: In the event of strong current or heavy storm activity the potential exists for the sediment tubes to be dislodged from the propeller scars, thereby negating any benefit. It is for this reason that securing the tubes with an anchoring pin and monitoring the stability of the tubes after a severe storm may be considered. There is the possibility that portions of the mesh tube could be dislodged during heavy storm events. As the material is designed to breakdown over a period of months, any such debris would be short-lived, thus minimizing it negative impact on the surrounding environment. In addition, anchor pins, if used, could contribute to marine debris.

4.7.1 Location and Area Uses (Sediment Tubes)

Direct Effects: No direct effects are expected.

Indirect Effects: Long-term minor beneficial indirect effects are expected. Since the sediment tubes will partially restore the site morphology, conditions will improve for seagrass recruitment and the return of associated flora, fauna, and recreational and/or commercial water based activities in the area.

4.7.2 Geology (Sediment Tubes)

Direct Effects: Long-term minor beneficial effects are expected as the placement of sediment tubes in the injured area will more quickly return the topography of the site to pre-grounding conditions. Short-term minor adverse effects on the topography could result from the disturbance of the substrate during restoration activities if proper mooring of work vessels is not maintained.

Indirect Effects: No indirect effects are expected.

4.7.3 Water Resources (Sediment Tubes)

Direct Effects: No direct effects are expected.

Indirect Effects: No indirect effects are expected.

4.7.4 Biological Resources (Sediment Tubes)

Direct Effects: The placement of sediment tubes will provide long-term direct benefits by providing a more suitable substratum for establishment of seagrasses. The food provision and nursery protection services the injured area provided to fish prior to injury will be more quickly restored. Additionally, seagreass transplants will permit the faster redevelopment of epiphytic and algal communities in the injured area. Endangered and threatened species would likely experience no direct effects.

Indirect Effects: Long-term minor beneficial effects on nearby seagrass and benthic animal communities are expected. The restoration benefits associated with sediment tubes are likely to lessen the chances of the surrounding communities being adversely affected by increased site erosion caused by high water current or annual storms. The eventual growth of benthic organisms, including algae, plus an increase in shelter habitat for juvenile fish, will provide additional food sources for fish living on or near the bank, including the larger predatory species that roam bank margins in search of prey. No indirect effects on endangered and threatened species are expected.

4.7.5 Infrastructure (Sediment Tubes)

Direct Effects: Short-term minor adverse effects are expected as a result of increased mooring activity and transportation movement.

Indirect Effects: No indirect effects are expected.

4.7.6 Hazardous and Toxic Substances (Sediment Tubes)

Direct Effects: No significant direct effects are expected. Restoration would not intentionally introduce significant new hazardous materials into the environment. The contractor will be required to address contingencies through plans needed for the permitting process. These would include incidental spillage of fuel.

Indirect Effects: No indirect effects are expected.

4.7.7 Socioeconomics (Sediment Tubes)

<u>Direct Effects:</u> No direct effects are expected.

<u>Indirect Effects:</u> Long-term minor beneficial effects are expected. By placing sediment tubes in the appropriate areas of the injury site, a better substrate for the establishment of seagrasses is created. Thus, it would lead to a slightly quicker recovery of seagrass and, in part, support the recreational and commercial marine related activities in the region.

4.7.8 Quality of Life (Sediment Tubes)

<u>Direct Effects:</u> No direct effects are expected

<u>Indirect Effects:</u> Long-term beneficial indirect effects are anticipated as successful restoration of the injured area will contribute in part toward an overall healthy seagrass ecosystem. This, in turn, helps support the viability of commercial and recreational activities that are directly or indirectly dependent on seagrass ecosystems.

4.8 BERM REDISTRIBUTION ALTERNATIVE

When appropriate, the redistribution (through raking or water-hosing) of the dislodged sediment back into the blowhole or propscar injury is a low-cost and effective restoration alternative. This alternative is suitable for shallow blowholes or propscars where the displaced sediment has formed a berm around the injury and workers can easily access the site. This restoration technique expedites recovery of the injured sites, resulting in direct and indirect ecological and socioeconomic benefits associated with healthy seagrass ecosystems.

Pros: This alternative directly addresses the potential instability of the injured areas by stabilizing the injury site, thereby facilitating conditions for a more rapid regrowth of seagrasses. Through the filling of blowholes or other injury features, the site can be modified to a state that is more similar to the pre-grounding conditions. Redistribution is beneficial in two major respects. First, it will advance the stabilization of the injury area, facilitating conditions for recovery. Second, berm redistribution will advance recovery of the seagrass that was previously buried by the berm material. In addition, the manual raking of sediment back into the injury features avoids the problem of potential additional injury due to the use of barge vessels and other mechanized equipment.

Cons: The redistribution of sediment fill may result in considerable immediate short-term turbidity as the sediment mix filters through the water to the injury basin. In areas with high tidal currents, finer sediments will disperse in the water column, potentially impacting neighboring seagrasses. In addition, for injury sites that have had rapid partial re-colonization, the sediment fill will smother any new growth. However, in many injured sites, the regrowth that occurs prior to restoration may not be stable, and thus not truly classified as "recovery" (Kenworthy 1998). The act of raking or water hosing may also injure any seagrass still surviving underneath the berm.

4.8.1 Location and Area Uses (Berm Redistribution)

<u>Direct Effects:</u> No direct effects are expected.

<u>Indirect Effects:</u> Long-term minor beneficial indirect effects are expected since the redistribution of the berms will at least partially restore the site morphology, and thus conditions amenable for seagrass recruitment and the return of associated flora and fauna. Recovery of the injury site will assist, in part, the continued viability of recreational and/or commercial activities dependent on healthy seagrass ecosystems.

4.8.2 Geology (Berm Redistribution)

Direct Effects: Long-term minor beneficial effects on geology will occur as a result of raking the berms into the injury features. A closer approximation to pre-grounding topography will help reestablish the pre-injury baseline conditions at the site.

Indirect Effects: No indirect effects are expected.

4.8.3 Water Resources (Berm Redistribution)

Direct Effects: Short-term minor adverse effects from increased turbidity generated during redistribution of sediment into the injured areas are expected. However, care will be taken to minimize these effects through the use of the most appropriate and cost effective technology. Long-term benefits in improved water quality are expected once seagrass re-colonize the injury area.

Indirect Effects: No indirect effects are expected.

4.8.4 Biological Resources (Berm Redistribution)

Direct Effects: The redistribution of sediment back into the injury area will provide long-term benefits for the re-colonization of the area by seagrasses. Seagrass re-colonization will directly and indirectly benefit numerous species of flora and fauna. The food provision and nursery protection services the injured area provided to fish prior to injury will be more quickly restored. Additionally, seagrass transplants will permit the faster redevelopment of epiphytic and algal communities in the injured area. Endangered and threatened species would likely experience no direct effects. In the event the seagrass injury is located within an area with known resident populations of manatees, restoration activities will be completed following state manatee protection guidelines ensuring their protection and minimization of overall disturbance.

Indirect Effects: Long-term minor beneficial effects on nearby seagrass and benthic animal communities are expected. The restoration of the injured area will lessen the chances of the surrounding communities being adversely affected by the forces exerted by annual storms, although dispersion of unconsolidated sediment out of the grounding area is still a possibility early in the recovery process.

Fish communities will experience long-term minor beneficial effects. The eventual growth of benthic organisms, including algae, plus an increase in shelter habitat for juvenile fish, will provide additional food sources for fish living on or near the injured area, including the larger predatory species that roam seagrass banks in search of prey. No indirect effects on endangered and threatened species are expected.

4.8.5 Infrastructure (Berm Redistribution)

Direct Effects: No direct effects are expected.

Indirect Effects: No indirect effects are expected.

4.8.6 Hazardous and Toxic Substances (Berm Redistribution)

Direct Effects: No adverse effects are expected. The contractor will be required to address contingencies through plans needed for the permitting process. These contingency plans will include incidental spillage of fuel.

Indirect Effects: No indirect effects are expected.

4.8.7 Socioeconomics (Berm Redistribution)

Direct Effects: No direct effects are expected.

Indirect Effects: Long-term minor beneficial effects are expected to occur as redistribution of fill will improve the likelihood of a successful seagrass restoration project, and, in part, an improvement in the seagrass ecology of the area. This in turn is positive for recreational and commercial activities that are directly and/or indirectly dependent on a healthy seagrass ecosystem.

4.8.8 Quality of Life (Berm Redistribution)

Direct Effects: No direct effects are expected.

Indirect Effects: Long-term beneficial indirect effects are anticipated as successful restoration of the injured area will contribute, in part, toward an overall healthy seagrass ecosystem. This, in turn, helps support the viability of commercial and recreational activities that are directly or indirectly dependent on seagrass ecosystems.

4.9 SOD REPLACEMENT ALTERNATIVE

When appropriate, large chunks of seagrasses with intact rhizomes may be placed back into a shallow propscar injury or blowhole. This alternative is suitable for shallow blowholes or propscars where additional sediment fill is not needed for the replaced seagrass to continue to thrive once replaced. This restoration technique expedites recovery of the injured sites, resulting in direct and indirect ecological and socioeconomic benefits associated with healthy seagrass ecosystems.

Pros: This alternative directly addresses the potential instability of the injured areas by giving the replaced sod a chance to thrive and stabilizing the injury site, thereby facilitating conditions for a more rapid regrowth of seagrasses.

Cons: There are no cons associated with this alternative.

4.9.1 Location and Area Uses (Sod Replacement)

Direct Effects: No direct effects are expected.

Indirect Effects: Long-term minor beneficial indirect effects are expected since the replacement of sod will at least partially restore the site morphology, and thus conditions amenable for seagrass recruitment and the return of associated flora and fauna. Recovery of the injury site will assist, in part, the continued viability of recreational and/or commercial activities dependent on healthy seagrass ecosystems.

4.9.2 Geology (Sod Replacement)

Direct Effects: Long-term minor beneficial effects on geology will occur as a result of placing sod in the injury features. This will decrease the probability of continued erosion.

Indirect Effects: No indirect effects are expected.

4.9.3 Water Resources (Sod Replacement)

Direct Effects: No direct effects are expected.

Indirect Effects: Sod replacement provides a minor long-term benefit by facilitating the growth and survival of seagrass that works to enhance water clarity and stabilize substrate, thus improving water quality.

4.9.4 Biological Resources (Sod Replacement)

Direct Effects: The replacement of intact sod into the injury area will provide long-term benefits for the re-colonization of the area by seagrasses. Seagrass re-colonization will directly benefit numerous species of flora and fauna. The food provision and nursery protection services the injured area provided to fish prior to injury will be more quickly restored. Additionally, seagreass transplants will permit the faster redevelopment of epiphytic and algal communities in the injured area. Endangered and threatened species would likely experience no direct effects.

Indirect Effects: Long-term minor beneficial effects on nearby seagrass and benthic animal communities are expected. The restoration of the injured area will lessen the chances of the surrounding communities being adversely affected by the forces exerted by annual storms.

Fish communities will experience long-term minor beneficial effects. The eventual growth of benthic organisms, including algae, plus an increase in shelter habitat for juvenile fish, will provide additional food sources for fish living on or near the injured area, including the larger predatory species that roam seagrass banks in search of prey. No indirect effects on endangered and threatened species are expected.

4.9.5 Infrastructure (Sod Replacement)

Direct Effects: No direct effects are expected.

Indirect Effects: No indirect effects are expected.

4.9.6 Hazardous and Toxic Substances (Sod Replacement)

Direct Effects: No direct effects are expected.

Indirect Effects: No indirect effects are expected.

4.9.7 Socioeconomics (Sod Replacement)

Direct Effects: No direct effects are expected.

Indirect Effects: Long-term minor beneficial effects are expected to occur as sod replacement will improve the likelihood of successful seagrass regrowth. In turn, this is positive for recreational and commercial activities that are directly and/or indirectly dependent on a healthy seagrass ecosystem.

4.9.8 Quality of Life (Sod Replacement)

Direct Effects: No direct effects are expected.

Indirect Effects: Long-term beneficial indirect effects are anticipated as successful restoration of the injured area will contribute, in part, toward an overall healthy seagrass ecosystem. This, in turn, helps support the viability of commercial and recreational activities that are directly or indirectly dependent on seagrass ecosystems.

4.10 EXCLUSION CAGE ALTERNATIVE

When injuries to seagrass beds occur near coral reefs, it is especially difficult for the seagrass to reestablish itself after restoration. A large variety of herbivores live in or frequent coral reefs and thus put abnormally high grazing pressure on nearby seagrass. Uninjured, well-established seagrass beds can sustain this pressure, but new transplants are quickly grazed to the point where they cannot sustain themselves because they are planted as smaller fragments or units, which are not as well integrated clonally as plants growing in an established meadow. However, research has shown that exclusion cages placed around new transplants for three to four months allow the beds to establish themselves to the point where they are sustainable after the cages are removed (Fonseca et al. 1994). Each exclusion cage must also be securely fastened to the substrate so that it does not become detached. This is particularly important in areas where cages are exposed to storm waves, ground swells, and other high-energy events.

Pros: This alternative directly addresses the survivability of seagrass transplants near coral reefs by protecting them from grazing by herbivores inhabiting the reef.

Cons: The possibility for vandalism exists. The possibility also exists for navigational incidents with the exclusion cages; however, this possibility is low as they are typically placed on the benthos in shallow water near reefs, which should not be regularly visited. There is also the possibility that cages exposed to storm waves, ground swells, and other high-energy events could become detached and float away. However, the cages are constructed and fastened to the substrate in such a way that this is unlikely. If cages were dislodged, it would be unlikely that restoration biologists could recover them; the cages would become long-lived contributions to marine debris.

4.10.1 Location and Area Uses (Exclusion Cages)

Direct Effects: In most instances, the impact on boaters will be limited as grounding locations are in shallow waters near coral reefs that should not be regularly visited.

Indirect Effects: Long-term minor beneficial indirect effects are expected, as exclusion cages will facilitate conditions amenable for seagrass recruitment and the return of associated fauna. It would be expected to hasten the return of recreational and/or commercial water based activities to the area.

4.10.2 Geology (Exclusion Cages)

Direct Effects: No direct effects are expected.

Indirect Effects: Long-term beneficial indirect effects are anticipated, as exclusion cages will facilitate seagrass growth and thus stabilization of the sediment in the injury area, thereby reducing the possibility of future site erosion.

4.10.3 Water Resources (Exclusion Cages)

Direct Effects: No direct effects on water quality or on the biological resources within the substrate that depend on high water quality are anticipated.

Indirect Effects: Exclusion cages facilitate the growth and survival of seagrass that enhances water clarity and stabilizes substrate, thus improving water quality.

4.10.4 Biological Resources (Exclusion Cages)

Direct Effects: Short and long term beneficial direct effects are anticipated for the seagrass communities. The construction of exclusion cages will provide long-term benefits for the re-colonization of the area by seagrasses. Seagrass re-colonization will directly benefit numerous species of flora and fauna. The food provision and nursery protection services the injured area provided to fish prior to injury will be more quickly restored. Additionally, seagreass transplants will permit the faster redevelopment of epiphytic and algal communities in the injured area. Endangered and threatened species would likely experience no direct effects.

Indirect Effects: Short and long term beneficial indirect effects are anticipated, as the recovery of the site will benefit seagrass dependent flora and fauna. By decreasing turbidity, the restored seagrass indirectly benefits both autotrophic and heterotrophic benthic organisms in nearby communities, including those found on associated coral reefs. Endangered and threatened species would likely experience no indirect effects.

4.10.5 Infrastructure (Exclusion Cages)

Direct Effects: Short-term minor adverse effects are expected as restoration activities will generate small increases in solid waste (refuse).

Indirect Effects: No indirect effects are expected.

4.10.6 Hazardous and Toxic Substances (Exclusion Cages)

Direct Effects: No direct effects are expected.

Indirect Effects: No indirect effects are expected.

4.10.7 Socioeconomics (Exclusion Cages)

Direct Effects: No direct effects are expected.

Indirect Effects: Long-term minor beneficial effects are expected. Restoring seagrass injuries in the Keys will support, in part, the continued growth of recreational and commercial marine related activities in the region.

4.10.8 Quality of Life (Exclusion Cages)

Direct Effects: No direct effects are expected.

Indirect Effects: Long-term beneficial indirect effects are anticipated as successful restoration of the injured area will contribute, in part, toward an overall healthy seagrass ecosystem. This, in turn, helps support the viability of commercial and recreational activities that are directly or indirectly dependent on seagrass ecosystems.

4.11 CUMULATIVE EFFECTS

Cumulative effects are those that result from the incremental effects of an action when considering past, present, and reasonably foreseeable near-term future actions, regardless of the agencies or parties involved. Cumulative effects can result from individually minor, but collectively significant factors taking place over time as they may relate to the entire region. The following sections summarize the potential cumulative effects for each action.

4.11.1 No Action Alternative

Several potential cumulative effects are associated with the no action alternative for seagrass restoration projects. No restoration action may lead to adverse effects on the immediate and surrounding areas. The original habitat (seagrass community) has been lost and therefore so have the functions associated with a seagrass ecosystem. Species diversity and composition in the immediate area have been lost and would not be replaced in the near future. Injured seagrass beds provide potential areas for the proliferation of unwanted species, such as filamentous and fleshy algae, which can then encroach on the surrounding seagrass meadows. Turbidity from loose sand and debris at the injured site may resuspend during storm activity, leading to potential adverse effects on surrounding seagrass communities and coral reefs. With the no action alternative, cumulatively, the aesthetic, recreational, and commercial value of the area may be reduced, resulting in a reduction in overall economic welfare. No action can also result in further degradation from future storm events.

4.11.2 Seagrass Transplant Alternative

The cumulative effect of seagrass transplants will be a more rapid return to pre-injury baseline environmental conditions. It is unlikely that the use of seagrass transplants alone will return the injured area to the pre-grounding topography of the area. Seagrass transplants will facilitate the re-establishment of seagrasses and stabilization of the surrounding injured substrate, thereby reducing the possibility for resuspension of sediment, additional site erosion, and collateral injury to neighboring seagrasses. Additionally, if not monitored, collection of seagrass transplants from donor sites could lead to degradation of those sites. Measures discussed previously will be taken to ensure that restoration actions do not harm donor sites.

4.11.3 Bird Stake Alternative

The cumulative effect of birdstakes will be a more rapid return to pre-injury baseline environmental conditions. It is unlikely that the use of bird stakes alone will return the injured area to pre-grounding topography of the area. Bird stakes will facilitate the re-establishment of seagrasses and stabilization of the surrounding injured substrate, thereby reducing the possibility for resuspension of sediment, additional site erosion, and collateral injury to neighboring seagrasses. Inevitably, some birdstakes will be vandalized or broken during storms; as such, lost birdstakes will contribute, in part, toward the larger problem of marine debris.

4.11.4 Fertilizer Spike Alternative

The cumulative effect of fertilizer spikes will be a more rapid return to pre-injury baseline environmental conditions. It is unlikely that the use of fertilizer spikes alone will return the injured area to pre-grounding topography of the area. Fertilizer spikes will facilitate the re-establishment of seagrasses and stabilization of the surrounding injured substrate as new seagrass initiates recovery. The return of seagrass in the injured area will reduce the possibility for resuspension of sediment, additional site erosion, and collateral injury to neighboring seagrasses. The short and long-term impacts of fertilizer spikes are viewed as positive toward recovery of the injured area and no negative direct or indirect effects are anticipated on the substrate or dependent organisms.

4.11.5 Sediment Fill Alternative

The cumulative effect of sediment fill will be a more rapid return to pre-injury baseline environmental conditions. The combination of sediment fill and re-colonizing seagrass will stabilize the injury site, thereby reducing the possibility for resuspension of sediment, additional site erosion, and collateral injury to neighboring seagrasses.

4.11.6 Sediment Tube Alternative

The cumulative effect of sediment tubes will be a more rapid return to pre-injury baseline environmental conditions at injury sites. Sediment tubes will facilitate the ability of seagrasses in the undisturbed side populations to naturally re-colonize the area. The combination of sediment tubes and re-colonizing seagrass will stabilize the injury site, thereby reducing the possibility for resuspension of sediment, additional site erosion, and collateral injury to neighboring seagrasses. In the event that the tube's mesh fabric is dislodged, it will contribute, in part, toward the larger problem of marine debris until it biodegrades.

4.11.7 Berm Redistribution Alternative

The cumulative effects of berm raking will result in short and long term beneficial impacts to the seagrass communities of the FKNMS. The benefits of berm raking will lead to a more expedited recovery of the seagrass injury and the seagrass bottom that was previously covered by the displaced sediment. Healthy seagrass communities are an essential component of the economic vitality of the commercial and recreational fishing and tourism industries in the FKNMS.

4.11.8 Sod Replacement Alternative

The cumulative effects of sod replacement will result in short and long term beneficial impacts to the seagrass communities of the FKNMS. The benefits of sod replacement will lead to a reversal of some of the injury by recreating pre-injury conditions. It will also allow biologists to avoid taking transplants from donor beds.

4.11.9 Exclusion Cage Alternative

The cumulative effect of exclusion cages will be a more rapid return to pre-injury baseline environmental conditions. It is unlikely that the use of exclusion cages alone will return the injured area to pre-grounding topography of the area. Exclusion cages will facilitate the re-establishment of seagrasses and stabilization of the surrounding injured substrate, thereby reducing the possibility for resuspension of sediment, additional site erosion, and collateral injury to neighboring seagrasses. Some exclusion cages may be swept away by storms and other high-energy events; as such, lost exclusion cages will contribute, in part, toward the larger problem of marine debris.

4.12 MITIGATION MEASURES

During the proposed restoration, the following mitigative measures would be undertaken to minimize the potential long-term and short-term adverse effects that could result from restoration activities.

4.12.1 Geology

Ensuring that vessels and equipment do not damage the existing seagrass meadows surrounding an injury site will reduce the potential for adverse effects. Work within the site area during darkness or periods of reduced visibility will not occur, and a foul weather and hurricane evacuation contingency plan will be developed to remove vessels from the area if changes in weather or sea-state conditions warrant.

4.12.2 Water Resources

Contractors will be required to comply with all applicable federal, state, and local regulations governing environmental pollution control and abatement. Turbidity controls and monitoring will take place during construction as appropriate and required.

4.12.3 Biological Resources

Contractors will employ all possible actions and strategies to minimize the impact of restoration actions on fish and wildlife. This includes instructing personnel on the proper procedures for conducting work in this type of habitat. Specifically, personnel should prevent any blockage to the movement of manatees or sea turtles in the environment, operate vessels at "no wake" speeds when in shallow waters, and temporarily delay work when manatees or sea turtles move within sight of the injury area. If the injury area is located in an area known to be an active mating, nesting, or nursery area for endangered species such as sea turtles or manatees, all actions must comply with state guidelines for manatee and sea turtle protection. Additionally, contractors will be required to comply with all applicable federal, state, and local regulations governing the protection of natural resources.

4.12.4 Infrastructure

Close coordination with Trustee personnel will be required with respect to the mooring of restoration-related vessels to avoid collateral injury to the seagrasses surrounding the injury area. Buoyant mooring lines will be used to keep the lines from striking the bottom during loading from wave action. Substantial anchors, placed off the seagrass beds in sand areas, may be necessary to resist wave-induced mooring loads. Adequate, approved disposal options will be made available for solid waste, with an emphasis on off-site/upland disposal. Additionally, there is potential for further injury to the seagrass meadows and the benthic environment from the movement of the sediment-carrying barges under the influence of swells. A storm-anchorage contingency plan will be established off-site if weather during the restoration forces the barges to move and take shelter. Supply vessels ferrying personnel and supplies to and from the restoration site create an increased potential for shallow bank strikes. Support vessels will use appropriate navigation and mooring techniques to reduce the possibility of additional injury to natural resources.

4.12.5 Cultural Resources

Should any cultural resources be discovered during restoration, work will be halted until appropriate State and Federal historic preservation officers are notified and authorization is granted to proceed with the restoration project.

4.12.6 Hazardous and Toxic Substances

Small petroleum, oil, or lubricant (POL) leaks may occur during restoration operations. Under normal conditions, these leaks or spills should be of insufficient volume to affect the sensitive habitat comprising the seagrass meadows and will likely evaporate or be washed away from the area. Only if a larger POL spill were to occur could there be a measurable impact on local communities. The likelihood of this type of spill is small overall due to the proper maintenance of restoration equipment. Additionally, the expected short duration of the immediate restoration activities would help to minimize the potential for a large release. Contractors will be required to comply with all applicable federal, state, and local regulations governing environmental pollution control and abatement.

4.13 SELECTION OF PREFERRED ALTERNATIVES

After consideration of the criteria for evaluating seagrass restoration options presented in Table 2-1, the description of the ten restoration options provided in chapter 2 (and summarized in Table 2-2), and the environmental and socioeconomic consequences detailed in this chapter, the following restoration options have been selected as the most preferred, depending on site-specific conditions:

1. *Seagrass Transplants*: Transplantation of *H. wrightii* or *S. filiforme* into the injury provides two distinct benefits. First, these faster growing, opportunistic species act to stabilize the injury site. This reduces the probability of injury expansion that may otherwise occur due to erosion, and facilitates the regrowth of the climax species, *T. testudinum*. Second, the transplants can immediately provide some of the environmental services that were lost as a result of the injury. While the benefits of the *H. wrightii* or *S. filiforme* transplants are certainly less than those that were provided by the mature seagrass community prior to grounding, they do represent an improvement over bare substratum. It is estimated that greater than 80% of restorations will include seagrass transplants.

2. *Bird Stakes*: It has been demonstrated that bird staking is an effective method to facilitate colonization of seagrasses into disturbed areas (Fourqurean et al. 1992a; Fourqurean et al. 1992b; Fourqurean et al. 1995; Kenworthy et al. 2000). Fertilizing significantly increases the success of transplanted *H. wrightii* and *S. filiforme*. Of the two restoration options that provide the nutrients necessary for successful transplantation, bird stakes are more cost-effective than fertilizer spikes. Stakes take advantage of a natural resource, birds, to provide concentrated doses of nutrients in the immediate vicinity of the injury. A concern with bird stakes is the possibility that they may be confused with navigational aids by boaters. The injury geometry will influence the likelihood of this misinterpretation. Prior to staking an injury, restoration biologists will weigh the restoration benefits with the potential impact on navigation. It is expected that bird stakes will be used at most restoration sites that are less than 1.5 meters in depth. Greater than 80% of restorations will likely include bird stakes.

3. *Sediment Fill*: Sediment fill is used to restore the natural gradient of the sea floor. By filling the site to grade, the probability that the injury will expand as the sides of the blowhole collapse is greatly reduced. Further, filling reduces the probability of injury expansion due to erosion. It is expected that sediment fill will be used for at many restoration sites where there is an escarpment of greater than 20 cm. It is estimated that approximately 50% of restorations will include sediment fill. The deeper (more severe) the blowhole, the greater the likelihood of using this restoration option.

These three preferred restoration options are not mutually exclusive. In fact, restoration of many sites will most effectively be accomplished by employing all three options. In addition, it must be recognized that the selection of these preferred options is based upon a "typical" injury. As such, the selection of these preferred options does not preclude the use of the other restoration technique at individual restoration sites. Depending on site-specific conditions, other techniques may be most appropriate. It is expected that fertilizer spikes, sediment tubes, berm redistribution, and exclusion cages will be included in less than 10% of restorations. Sod replacement will always be undertaken when feasible, however, it is expected to be included in less than 20% of restorations.

4.14 CONCLUSIONS

The proposed actions to restore seagrass injuries in the FKNMS have been analyzed by comparing the environmental and socioeconomic effects associated with the range of potential restoration alternatives. Baseline environmental and socioeconomic conditions for areas subject to potential seagrass injuries in the FKNMS and the region of influence have been described, and the environmental and socioeconomic consequences of implementing the proposed actions evaluated. The analysis shows that, unless noted in a separate document, the environmental and socioeconomic conditions at the grounding sites will not be significantly affected in a negative way by proceeding with any of the restoration alternatives discussed.

CHAPTER 5. THE SEAGRASS REGIONAL RESTORATION PLAN

5.1 PURPOSES OF THE REGIONAL RESTORATION PLAN

The purposes of the regional restoration plan are to outline the criteria used for the selection of compensatory restoration areas and to identify specific candidate areas. In addition to primary restoration of the site injured by a vessel grounding, natural resource damage assessment (NRDA) claims include a compensatory restoration component. Compensatory restoration is required to compensate the public for lost interim ecological resources and services from the time of initial injury until full recovery of the injured (primary) site. The basis for determining the appropriate scale of compensatory seagrass restoration is derived from biological and economic models that estimate the amount of seagrass services lost and time to full recovery (Fonseca et al. 2000). Funds collected from compensatory restoration components of NRDA cases will be used to implement restoration as described in this regional restoration plan.

To maximize the restoration impact, compensatory funds collected from small seagrass NRDA cases will be pooled to allow the implementation of larger seagrass restoration projects. This permits NOAA and the State of Florida to capitalize on economies of scale in restoration. Funds may also be used for the implementation of seagrass injury prevention projects. All compensatory restoration projects will focus on seagrass restoration and injury prevention projects within the FKNMS.

5.2 REGIONAL RESTORATION AND INJURY PREVENTION PROJECTS

Compensatory restoration is one component of this regional restoration plan. In addition to grounding injuries that have identified responsible parties, there are many other grounding injuries discovered each year. Because those responsible for causing these injuries are unidentified, the locations are referred to as "orphan" sites. Each of the potential geographic areas discussed in this chapter has a large number of orphan seagrass injuries that would benefit from restoration. These are the areas that the regional restoration plan seeks to address.

Preventive projects are the second component of the regional restoration plan. Preventive projects seek to reduce the frequency of vessel groundings, thereby decreasing the amount of area that requires restoration in the future. Boater education campaigns and the posting of informative signs at boat ramps, marinas, and fuel depots are examples of preventive projects that might be considered under the regional restoration plan. In addition, the use of water markers to alert boaters to hazards is a potentially attractive use of compensatory funds.

Water markers are aides to navigation, such as channel and shoal markers and regulatory signs, that assist boaters to safely navigate the treacherous shoals and difficult channels of shallow Florida Keys waterways. These devices help to prevent natural resource injury as these waterway markers direct boaters to use the deep water of navigation channels instead of the shallow seagrass flats, banks, and shoals where the potential for running aground is high. Regulatory signs for no motor zones are an attempt to prevent boaters from entering and injuring shallow seagrass flats with high wildlife habitat value. Regulatory signs for idle speed or no wake zones endeavor to prevent boats from disturbing shoreline vegetation and resuspending sediments with their wakes.

In shallow water environments that have been identified as highly impacted from vessel groundings, waterway markers may be installed to reduce natural resource injuries and allow for the restoration of disturbed natural communities. Prior to installing markers, all issues related to the size, location, and expected lifetime will be approved by all appropriate and necessary agencies. The use of waterway marking as an injury prevention tool must also consider maintenance and operational issues. Additionally, if water markers are used over aggressively, or if they are placed too close to the bank, they can become confusing for mariners, thus causing more degradation as boaters ground on the bank. Depending on the viewer, they may be considered a form of visual pollution.

5.3 SELECTION OF PRIORITY AREAS

To implement the regional restoration plan, NOAA and the State of Florida have divided the FKNMS into three regions. The Upper Keys region spans Key Largo through Channel Five Bridge; the Middle Keys region from the Channel Five Bridge to Niles Channel; and the Lower Keys region from Niles Channel south and west through the remainder of the FKNMS to the Dry Tortugas. Figure 5-1 illustrates these divisions. The compensatory funds obtained from NRDA cases in each region will usually be put toward compensatory restoration in that same region.[3] However, in circumstances in which resource managers feel it is appropriate, injury sites located outside the region from which compensatory funds derive may be selected.

Pairing the goal of maximizing economies of scale in restoration with the desire to create a viable compensatory restoration project in each region, the regional restoration plan seeks to identify one area within each of the three FKNMS regions for restoration implementation. The three areas selected will be those in which the frequency of groundings is high and various factors indicate that restoration will be successful.

Figure 5-1. Frequently injured seagrass areas within the Florida Keys National Marine Sanctuary

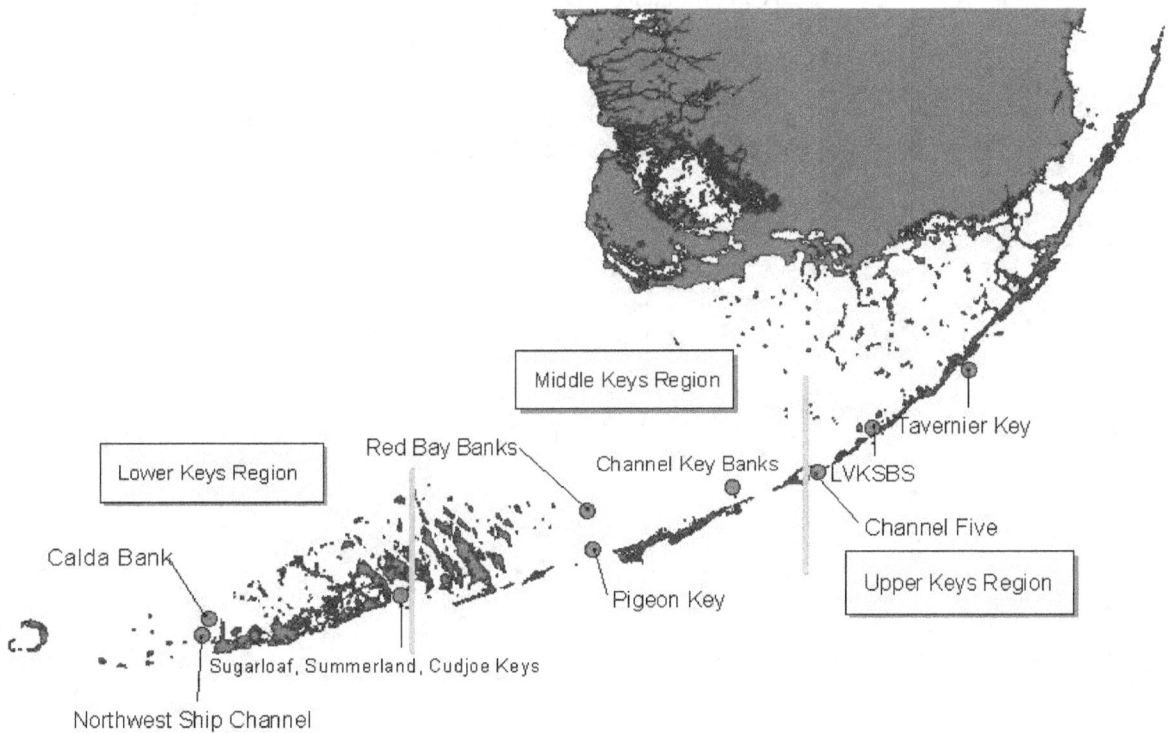

---

[3] Funds recovered for injuries to resources within state parks will be put towards compensatory restoration in that same park.

5.3.1 Statistical Analysis of Grounding Frequency Data by Region

While injuries to seagrass beds are widespread, they are not uniform in distribution. Some geographical areas are more heavily impacted than others. To prioritize potential locations for restoration using compensatory funds, the frequency of grounding events by area is an important initial consideration. It is believed that groundings in the most frequently injured areas will decline by working to change human behavior through public outreach, education, and potential changes to navigational aids associated with a regional restoration project site.

Available seagrass grounding data was used to mathematically determine areas in each FKNMS region that receive disproportionate injuries from vessels.[4] Each grounding incident was assigned to an area using GPS coordinates or detailed geographic description. An area is defined as a small subsection of a region, usually consisting of a few square kilometers, (e.g. Red Bay Banks, Tavernier Key Bank, Middle Grounds, etc.).[5] Once all grounding incidents were assigned areas, the number of groundings in each area was divided by the total number of groundings within the FKNMS. This produced a percentage of groundings for each area. This calculation was made according to the formula,

$$P_i = [(G_i \, / \, T_g)*100]$$

where,

P_i = percentage of groundings in area i
G_i = number of groundings within area i
T_g = total grounding events in FKNMS.

The ten most frequently impacted areas within each region are listed in Tables 5-1 through 5-3. The location of the three most frequently injured areas in each region is shown in Figure 5-1.

---

[4] Data used in this analysis reflects FKNMS records as of October 10, 2001.
[5] Each of these areas is clearly marked on NOAA navigational charts.

Table 5-1: Upper Keys Region Most Frequently Injured Areas

Area	Percent of Total FKNMS Groundings
Lignumvitae (LVKSBS)	11%
Tavernier Key	6.5%
Channel Five (Oceanside/Jewfish Hole Bank)	6.0%
Whale Harbor	3.5%
Snake Creek	3.5%
Cotton Key	3.0%
Tarpon Basin	1.5%
Port Largo Canal	1.0%
Broad Creek	0.5%
Indian Waterway	0.5%

Table 5-2: Middle Keys Region Most Frequently Injured Areas

Area	Percent of Total FKNMS Groundings
Red Bay Bank	6.0%
Pigeon Key	4.0%
Bethel Bank	3.0%
Looe Key	3.0%
Channel Key Pass/Banks	2.5%
Stirrup Key	1.5%
Yacht Channel	1.5%
Money Key	1.5%
Sprigger Bank	1.0%
Rachel Banks	1.0%

Table 5-3: Lower Keys Region Most Frequently Injured Areas

Area	Percent of Total FKNMS Groundings
NW Ship Channel	5.0%
Cudjoe/Summerland/Sugarloaf Key	3.5%
Calda Bank	3.0%
Boca Grande	3.0%
Lakes Entrance	2.0%
Boca Chica Channel	2.0%
Key West Harbor	1.5%
Marquesa Keys	1.5%
Middle Grounds	0.5%
Channel Key	0.5%

5.3.2 Evaluation of Priority Areas for Regional Restoration Action

After determining the distribution of injuries, a multi-category evaluation system was developed to prioritize regional restoration areas in the Upper, Middle, and Lower Keys regions. As a starting point, the top three statistically most injured areas in each of the three regions were considered for restoration with compensatory funds. These nine areas were compared based on four evaluation criteria. All areas were ranked with a score of either one or zero. Across all of the criteria, the accumulation of points was viewed as a positive indication that the site is a high priority for restoration action. Each site criterion considered is defined below[6]. The evaluation scoring is summarized in Table 5-4.

1. **Frequency of Injury:** It is believed that the publicity surrounding the designation of an area as a regional restoration area will result in heightened public awareness of the problem of vessel groundings in the area. An area designated as a regional restoration site may be more likely to receive additional navigational aids, patrols, and signs for boaters (injury prevention measures). Additionally, the placement of birdstakes, which will be observable at many of the restoration sites, will help raise awareness of the problem. *Scoring: If an area has the highest frequency of groundings per regional zone (Upper, Middle, and Lower Keys) it receives a one, otherwise, a zero.*

2. **Proximity to Land:** All other factors being equal, if an injury area is within five kilometers of shore, restoration field logistics and monitoring will be facilitated due to the area's accessibility. Proximity to land is especially important during inclement weather. *Scoring: If an area is within 5 km of shore it receives a one, otherwise, a zero.*

3. **No Motor Zone:** All other factors being equal, areas that are designated no-motor zones have a lower risk of re-injury from new boat groundings once a restoration project is implemented. Because the regional restoration plan seeks to identify and restore areas where the likelihood of long-term success is greatest, no-motor zones fall higher on the priority list. *Scoring: If an area is within a no-motor zone it receives a one, otherwise, zero.*

4. **Jurisdiction:** As the implementation of these regional restoration projects is a joint NOAA and State of Florida endeavor, it is anticipated that the permitting and management oversight of a restoration project will be more efficient if it occurs in an area with no other overlapping jurisdictions with local, state and federal government agencies.[7] *Scoring: If an area is within the jurisdiction of NOAA and FDEP with no other overlapping local, state, or federal agency jurisdictions, it receives a one, otherwise, a zero.*

---

[6] All of these criteria may be determined by non-field data, except for frequency of injury.

[7] This "jurisdiction" criterion shall not be construed to apply to use of funds recovered for injuries to resources within state parks. Except for reimbursement of response and assessment costs, pursuant to the Agreement for Coordination of Civil Claims between NOAA and the Board of Trustees of the Internal Improvement Trust Fund of the State of Florida, funds recovered for injured Sanctuary resources within a state park that is within the FKNMS shall be used to restore, manage, and improve that state park.

Table 5-4. Criteria for Selection of Seagrass RRP Project Sites

	Frequency of Injury	Proximity to Land	No Motor Zone	Jurisdiction	Total
UPPER KEYS					
Tavernier Key	0	1	1	1	3
LVKSBS	1	1	1	0	3
Channel Five	0	1	0	1	2
MIDDLE KEYS					
Pigeon Key	0	1	0	1	2
Bethel Bank	0	1	0	1	2
Red Bay Bank	1	0	0	1	2
LOWER KEYS					
Cudjoe Key	0	1	0	1	2
Calda Bank	0	0	0	1	1
NW Ship Channel	1	0	0	1	2

Based on the analysis of the most frequently injured areas in the Upper, Middle, and Lower Keys regions and the selection criteria scores in Table 5-4, the following locations have been selected as priority areas for regional restoration projects. Among areas with equal score totals, those areas that were considered most cost-effective to restore were selected.

Upper Keys: Tavernier Key and LVKSBS

Middle Keys: Pigeon Key

Lower Keys: Cudjoe Key

NOAA and the State of Florida reserve the right to deviate from these selected areas so long as a strong nexus with the injured resources and services is maintained.

5.4 ASSESSMENT OF SELECTED AREAS

Data on orphan injury sites in the selected areas were compiled using aerial photos and on-site visits. NOAA and the State of Florida examined the individual grounding sites in each area and chose those with the greatest probability of successful restoration. Once the individual orphan sites were selected for restoration, NOAA and the State of Florida conducted detailed on-scene injury assessments of each site to document the size and severity of the injury. The injury assessment for a representative orphan site can be found in Appendix A. Additional sites from the priority list will be selected and assessed in the future as compensatory funds accumulate.

5.5 MONITORING OF REGIONAL RESTORATION ACTIONS

Monitoring of the compensatory restoration projects is necessary to determine whether they are providing services in a manner consistent with restoration goals and to assess the potential need for mid-course corrections to ensure that the projects meet designated restoration performance standards. This monitoring is similar in scope, though larger in scale, than the monitoring required for primary restoration of seagrass injuries with identified responsible parties. The design of the monitoring program permits the detection of, and response to, significant changes in seagrass recovery rates or damage to restoration components (bird stakes, seagrass transplants, sediment fill, etc.) as a result of external events, such as major storms or vandalism. Eight monitoring events will be completed at each restoration site over a five-year period. A detailed discussion of the steps involved in each monitoring event can be found in Appendix A.

5.6 SEAGRASS EXPERTS CONTACTED

The following list of seagrass managers and experts were contacted during the formation of this regional restoration plan:

Richard Butgereit, Aug. 20, 2002.

John Dotten, Environmental Specialist II, Florida Keys National Marine Sanctuary, July 26, 2001; Aug. 21, 2002.

Michael R, Johnson, Fishery Biologist, National Marine Fisheries Service, July 17, 2001; Aug. 19, 2002.

Rich Jones, Marine Resources Planner, Monroe County Marine Resources, July 25, 2001.

Jud Kenworthy, Seagrass Biologist, National Oceanic and Atmospheric Administration (NOAA), various dates.

Kevin Kirsch, Seagrass Biologist, National Oceanic and Atmospheric Administration (NOAA), various dates.

Curtis Kruer, Aug. 1, 2002.

Lauri MacLaughlin, Sanctuary Resources Specialist, FKNMS, July 2001 (and other dates).

Anne McCarthy, Environmental Specialist III, FDEP/FKNMS and Lower Region Manager, Florida Keys National Marine Sanctuary, July 27, 2001 (and other dates).

Patricia McNeese, Environmental Consultant, June 24, 2002 (and other dates).

Sean Meehan, Seagrass Biologist, National Oceanic and Atmospheric Administration (NOAA), various dates.

Jerald Morrison, Environmental Consultant, Aug. 21, 2002.

Bill Sargent, FMRI Research Scientist, Aug. 21, 2002.

Lt. Joe Scarpa, Law Enforcement Officer, Florida Fish and Wildlife Commission, August 2001.

Officer Greg Stanley, Law Enforcement Officer, Florida Fish and Wildlife Commission, September 2001.

Pat Wells, Park Manager II, Lignumvitae Key State Botanical Site/ Monroe County Port Commission Chairman, October 17, 2001; June 21, 2002.

CHAPTER 6. RELATIONSHIP TO OTHER LAWS AND PROGRAMS

The implementation of the restoration alternatives require the Trustees to obtain proper work permits, comply with the provisions of federal and state regulations, and notify appropriate organizations before conducting any restoration activity. This PEIS serves as the primary document to communicate to the public the proposed criteria for restoration consideration, restoration alternatives, and anticipated restoration impacts.

6.1 NATIONAL ENVIRONMENTAL POLICY ACT OF 1969 (Public Law 91-190)

This document has been prepared in accordance with NEPA requirements. The purpose of this document is to assist in determining whether the proposed federal actions will have significant impacts on the quality of the human environment.

6.2 NOAA ADMINISTRATIVE ORDER ON ENVIRONMENTAL REVIEW PROCEDURES (NAO 216-6)

NOAA Administrative Order 216-6 requires that all proposed Federal projects be reviewed for their environmental consequences on the human environment. This review must result in the issuance of an Environmental Impact Statement (EIS), an Environmental Assessment (EA) with a Finding of No Significant Impact (FONSI), or a Categorical Exclusion (CE). It is anticipated that the types of seagrass restoration projects described in this PEIS are eligible for CEs from an EA because the actions meet the following criteria set forth in NAO 216-6 §6.03.b.2. The actions:

1) are intended to restore an ecosystem, habitat, biotic community, or population of living resources to a determinable pre-impact condition;
2) use for transplant only organisms currently or formerly present at the site or in its immediate vicinity;
3) do not require substantial dredging, excavation, or placement of fill; and
4) do not involve a significant added risk of human or environmental exposure to toxic or hazardous substances.

Consistent with these criteria, the purpose of seagrass restoration is to return seagrass habitat to pre-grounding conditions. With regard to the preferred restoration options selected in this PEIS, seagrass transplants will be taken from donor sites proximate to the injury areas, the placement of fill will be minimal and is necessary for seagrass reestablishment, and there is no added risk of human or environmental exposure to toxic or hazardous substances as a result of the restoration. Furthermore, the on-site, in-kind restoration of seagrass meadows is specifically mentioned in the NOAA NEPA guidance as an example action eligible for categorical exclusion (NAO 216-6).

The actions described in this PEIS to address injuries from small vessel groundings do not individually or cumulatively pose significant impacts on the human environment, and, therefore, are likely categorically excluded from an Environmental Assessment.

Prior to implementing restoration at each vessel grounding site, NOAA will prepare the information necessary to support a categorical exclusion determination, including site specific restoration plans. This documentation will be provided to NOAA's NEPA Coordinator for review. If the NEPA Coordinator determines that the action does not qualify for a CE, an EA will be conducted in accordance with NAO 216-6 and NEPA. Because of the frequency of vessel groundings and the similarity of site-specific preferred restoration options, several individual restoration projects may be included in the same categorical exclusion review. Regardless of whether restorations are subjected to categorical exclusion review individually or as part of a group of projects, each site will have an individual restoration plan drafted.

6.3 NATIONAL MARINE SANCTUARIES ACT (16 U.S.C. Sec. 1431 et seq., as amended)

As required by the National Marine Sanctuaries Act (NMSA) (also known as Title III of the Marine Protection, Research, and Sanctuaries Act of 1972), NOAA will expend settlement monies toward restoration of the injured sites and on seagrass injury prevention actions. The restoration alternatives and injury prevention actions proposed in this PEIS represent the preferred alternatives identified by the Trustees. Under Section 312, the NMSA stipulates that recovered amounts in excess of those required to be expended for response costs and damage assessments, must be used, in order of priority, to restore, replace, or acquire the equivalent of the sanctuary resources where the subject resources are located and to manage and improve any other national marine sanctuary. Amounts recovered for injuries to sanctuary resources lying within the jurisdiction of the State of Florida must be used in accordance with the Agreement for the Coordination of Civil Claims between NOAA and the Board of Trustees of the Internal Improvement Trust Fund of the State of Florida.

6.4 FLORIDA KEYS NATIONAL MARINE SANCTUARY AND PROTECTION ACT (Public Law 101-605)

The Florida Keys Marine Sanctuary and Protection Act requires that NOAA coordinate with the appropriate federal, state, and local governmental agencies and entities to support implementation of the Sanctuary management plan. The proposed actions analyzed in this document will occur within the boundaries of the FKNMS, and therefore NOAA will ensure that all activities comply with the Sanctuary management plan.

6.5 CLEAN WATER ACT (33 U.S.C. Sec. 1251 et seq.)

When restoration is in state waters and requires sediment fill, NOAA will submit a Joint Application for Works in the Waters of Florida to federal and state authorities to obtain permission under the Army Corps of Engineers Nationwide Permit 32.

6.6 COASTAL ZONE MANAGEMENT CONSISTENCY (16 U.S.C. Sec. 1451 et seq.)

When restoration actions may affect the State of Florida coastal zone, NOAA will obtain consistency certification under the Coastal Zone Management Act (CZMA). Consistency certification will be obtained through federal consistency review of this document and through a State Environmental Resource Permit (ERP) review. ERP review, which includes Florida Coastal Management Program agency review and approval of the Clean Water Act water quality certification, may constitute a consistency determination by the State of Florida.

6.7 ENDANGERED SPECIES ACT (16 U.S.C. §§ 1531-1543)

If NOAA trustees determine that site-specific restoration actions may adversely affect listed endangered or threatened species, consultation will be conducted pursuant to Section 7 of the Endangered Species Act. All rules and penalties governing this act will apply.

6.8 MAGNUSON-STEVENS FISHERY CONSERVATION AND MANAGEMENT ACT (Public Law 94-265, as amended)

The Magnuson-Stevens Act requires that the regional Fishery Management Councils identify essential fish habitat (EFH). Once designated, the Act requires all federal agencies to consult with the National Marine Fisheries Service (now NOAA Fisheries) when any activity proposed to be permitted, funded, or undertaken may have adverse effects on EFH. Consultation is not required if the federal agency determines that adverse impacts to EFH will not occur. Restoration activities that result in the conversion of habitat from one type to another type, when both types are designated as EFH, will result in a permanent adverse impact on the original EFH type. Consultation would be necessary for such restoration actions.

The seagrass restoration actions described in this document are designed to restore seagrass EFH in those areas that supported seagrass EFH prior to grounding-associated injuries. Therefore, there will be no conversion from one EFH habitat type to another type; simply a replacement of what once was present. In addition, as described in chapters 3 and 4, it is anticipated that the restoration techniques to be employed will not result in any adverse impacts to other EFH types. Therefore, EFH assessments and consultation with NOAA Fisheries will not be required for most restoration activities. If, however, the Trustees determine that site-specific restoration recommendations may endanger other EFH types, consultation will occur in accordance with the Act. If consultation is required, individuals from the federal Office of National Marine Sanctuaries will initiate discussions with NOAA Fisheries.

6.9 FLORIDA DEPARTMENT OF ENVIRONMENTAL PROTECTION, BUREAU ON INVASIVE PLANT MANAGEMENT

Under Chapter 369, Florida Statutes, the harvest and transport of aquatic plants from state sovereign submerged lands are prohibited unless a permit is granted. When restoration actions require the collection and transplantation of seagrasses, an aquatic plant collection permit will be obtained.

6.10 FLORIDA DEPARTMENT OF ENVIRONMENTAL PROTECTION, BUREAU OF SUBMERGED LANDS AND ENVIRONMENTAL RESOURCES

Under state law, Florida has jurisdiction over dredge and fill operations in or connected to waters of the state. In addition to water quality certification, an environmental resource permit will provide approval for activities conducted on state sovereign submerged lands.

6.11 FLORIDA DEPARTMENT OF STATE, DIVISION OF HISTROICAL RESOURCES

The Division of Historical Resources' State Historic Preservation Officer (SHPO) will be contacted to confirm the presence or absence of known archaeological or historical sites.

6.12 MONROE AND DADE COUNTY DEPARTMENTS OF ENVIRONMENTAL RESOURCE MANAGEMENT

Permits for restoration actions within the jurisdiction of Monroe County, Florida will be secured. If lime rock for the restoration is taken from Dade County, NOAA will consult with the Dade County Department of Environmental Resource Management regarding environmental requirements.

6.13 UNITED STATES COAST GUARD

NOAA will notify the Coast Guard concerning the nature and timing of restoration activities so that the Coast Guard can issue a notice to mariners.

CHAPTER 7. LIST OF PREPARERS

The following individuals contributed to writing this PEIS:

Kim Barry, Economist, Damage Assessment Center, Office of Response and Restoration, National Ocean Service, National Oceanic and Atmospheric Administration

Mark Fonseca, Research Team Leader, Center for Coastal Fisheries and Habitat Research, National Ocean Service, National Oceanic and Atmospheric Administration

Toben Galvin, Economist, Damage Assessment Center, Office of Response and Restoration, National Ocean Service, National Oceanic and Atmospheric Administration

Kamille Hammerstrom, Researcher, NOAA, Center for Coastal Fisheries and Habitat Research, National Ocean Service, National Oceanic and Atmospheric Administration.

Charles Jabaly, South Florida Aquatic Preserve Manager, Florida Department of Environmental Protection

Brian Julius, Gulf Branch Chief, Damage Assessment Center, Office of Response and Restoration, National Ocean Service, National Oceanic and Atmospheric Administration

Jud Kenworthy, Research Team Leader, Center for Coastal Fisheries and Habitat Research, National Ocean Service, National Oceanic and Atmospheric Administration

Anne McCarthy, Environmental Administrator, Lower Keys Region Manager, Florida Keys National Marine Sanctuary, Florida Department of Environmental Protection

Harriet Sopher, Resource Protection Program Manager, National Marine Sanctuaries Division, Office of Ocean and Coastal Resource Management, National Ocean Service, National Oceanic and Atmospheric Administration

Alice Stratton, Ecologist, Resources Protection Team, National Marine Sanctuaries Division, Office of Ocean and Coastal Resource Management, National Ocean Service, National Oceanic and Atmospheric Administration

Lisa Symons, Resource Protection and Damage Assessment Coordinator, National Marine Sanctuaries Division, Office of Ocean and Coastal Resource Management, National Ocean Service, National Oceanic and Atmospheric Administration

Steve Thur, Economist, Damage Assessment Center, Office of Response and Restoration, National Ocean Service, National Oceanic and Atmospheric Administration

Bruce Terrell, Cultural Resources Coordinator, National Marine Sanctuaries Division, Office of Ocean and Coastal Resource Management, National Ocean Service, National Oceanic and Atmospheric Administration

Fritz Wettstein, Lower Keys Regional Manager, Florida Keys National Marine Sanctuary, Florida Department of Environmental Protection

Paula Whitfield, Researcher, Center for Coastal Fisheries and Habitat Research, National Ocean Service, National Oceanic and Atmospheric Administration

CHAPTER 8. REFERENCES

Acosta, A, T Dunmire and J Venier (1998). "A Preliminary Trophic Model of the Fish Communities of Florida Bay". In *Proceedings: 1998 Florida Bay Science Conference*. May 12-14, 1998, R. J. Brock, S. H. Taylor, and P. Wingrove, eds. University of Miami, Florida Sea Grant College Program.

Chiappone, M and KM Sullivan (1996). <u>Functional Ecology and Ecosystem Trophodynamics: Site Characterization for the Florida Keys National Marine Sanctuary and Environs</u>. Volume 8. The Nature Conservancy, Zenda, WI.

Continental Shelf Associates, Inc. (1990). "Synthesis of Available Biological, Geological, Chemical, Socioeconomic, and Cultural Resource Information of the South Florida Area". MMS 90-0019. Prepared for U.S. Department of the Interior, Minerals Management Service. New Orleans, Louisiana.

Dawes, CJ (1987). "The Dynamic Seagrasses of the Gulf of Mexico and Florida Coasts". In *Proceedings of the Symposium on Subtropical-Tropical Seagrasses of the Southeastern United States*. MJ Durako, RC Phillips, and RR Lewis, III, eds. Florida Marine Research Publications, 42:25-38.

Dennison, WC, RJ Orth, KA Moore, JC Stevenson, V Carter, S Kollar, PW Bergstrom, and RA Batiuk (1993). "Assessing Water Quality with Submerged Aquatic Vegetation". *BioScience*. 43(2):86-94.

Durako, MJ and MD Moffler (1984). "Qualitative assessment of five artificial growth media on growth and survival of *Thalassia testudinum (Hydrocharitaceae)* seedlings". In FJ Webb, ed. *Proc. 11th Ann. Conf. Wetland Restoration and Creation*. p 73-92. Hillsborough Community College, Tampa, FL.

Duarte, CM and J Cebrian (1996). "The fate of marine autotrophic production". *Limnology and Oceanography*. 41:1758-66.

English, DB, W Kriesel, VR Leeworthy, and PC Wiley (1996). "Economic Contribution of Recreating Visitors to the Florida Keys/Key West". National Oceanic and Atmospheric Administration. Washington, D. C.

Enos, P (1997). "Holocene Sediment Accumulations of the South Florida Shelf Margin". In <u>Quaternary Sedimentation in South Florida</u>, Part 1, P Enos and RD Perkins, eds. pp. 1-130. Geological Society of America Memoir Number 147. Geological Society of America, Boulder, Colorado.

Florida Fish and Wildlife Conservation Commission (FFWCC) (2004). "Florida's Endangered Species, Threatened Species, and Species of Special Concern". January 29, 2004. Available at http://www.wildflorida.org/species/Endangered-Threatened-Special-Concern-2004.pdf. Accessed on July 23, 2004.

Florida Keys National Marine Sanctuary (1996). Final Management Plan / Environmental Impact Statement. National Oceanic and Atmospheric Administration. Silver Spring, MD.

Fonseca, MS (1990). "Regional Analysis of the Creation and Restoration of Seagrass Systems". In <u>Wetland Creation and Restoration: The Status of the Science</u>. JA Kusler and ME Kentula, eds. Island Press, Washington, DC.

Fonseca MS, WJ Kenworthy, GW Thayer (1998). <u>Guidelines for the Conservation and Restoration of Seagrasses in the United States and Adjacent Waters</u>. NOAA Coastal Ocean Program Decision Analysis Series No. 12. NOAA Coastal Ocean Office, Silver Spring, MD: 222pp. http://shrimp.ccfhrb.noaa.gov/library/digital.html.

Fonseca, MS, BE Julius, and WJ Kenworthy (2000). "Integrating Biology and Economics in Seagrass Restoration: How Much is Enough and Why?". *Ecological Engineering*. 15: 227-37.

Fourqurean, J and J Zieman (1991). "Photosynthesis, respiration and whole plant carbon budget of the seagrass *Thalassia testudinum*". *Marine Ecology Progress Series*. 69:161-70.

Fourqurean JW, JC Zieman, and GVN Powell (1992a). "Relationships between porewater nutrients and seagrasses in a subtropical carbonate environment". *Mar. Biol*. 114:57-65.

Fourqurean JW, JC Zieman, and GVN Powell (1992b). "Phosphorus limitation of primary production in Florida Bay: evidence from the C:N:P rations of the dominant seagrass *Thalassia testudinum*". *Limnology and. Oceanography*. 37:162-71.

Fourqurean JW, GVN Powell, WJ Kenworthy, and JC Zieman (1995). "The effects of long-term manipulation of nutrient supply on competition between the seagrasses *Thalassia testudinum* and *Halodule wrightii* in Florida Bay". *Oikos* 72:349-58.

Fourqurean, A, CD Willsie, CD Rose, and LM Rutten (2001). "Spatial and temporal patterns in seagrass community composition and productivity in south Florida". *Mar. Biol* 138:341-54.

Forqurean, JW, MJ Durako, JC Zieman (2001). "Seagrass Monitoring in the Florida Keys National Marine Sanctuary". Executive Summary, Annual Report FY 2001. http://serc.fiu.edu/seagrass/ExecutiveSummary01.htm.

Gallegos, CL and WJ Kenworthy (1996). "Seagrass depth limits in the Indian River Lagoon (Florida, U.S.A.): Application of an optical water quality model". *Estuar. Coast. Shelf Sci*. 42:267-88.

Hemminga, M and C Duarte (2000). Seagrass Ecology. Cambridge University Press. Cambridge, UK.

Iverson, RL and HF Bittaker (1986). "Seagrass distribution and abundance in eastern Gulf of Mexico coastal waters". *Estuarine and Coastal Shelf Science*. 22:577-602.

Kenworthy, WJ and DE Haunert (eds.) (1991). "The light requirements of seagrasses: proceedings of a workshop to examine the capability of water quality criteria, standards and monitoring programs to protect seagrasses". National Oceanic and Atmospheric Administration Technical Memorandum, National Marine Fisheries Service, Southeast Fisheries Science Center-287. Beaufort, North Carolina.

Kenworthy, WJ and MS Fonseca. (1996). "Light requirements of seagrasses Halodule wrightii and Syringodium filiforme derived from the relationship between diffuse light attenuation and maximum depth distribution". *Estuaries* 19:740-50.

Kenworthy, WJ and PW Whitfield (1998). "*Captain Joe* Grounding Site Survey: Post Hurricane Georges". National Oceanic and Atmospheric Administration. Beaufort Laboratory. Beaufort, North Carolina.

Kenworthy, WJ, MS Fonseca, PW Whitfield, KK Hammerstrom. and Schwartzschild (2000). "A Comparison of Two Methods for Enhancing the Recovery of Seagrasses into Propeller Scars: Mechanical Injection of a Nutrient and Growth Hormone Solution vs. Defecation by Roosting Seabirds". Final Report Submitted to the Florida Keys Environmental Restoration Trust Fund. Located at http://shrimp.bea.nmfs.gov/~mfonseca/lvfinalreport.pdf).

Kenworthy, WJ, MS Fonseca, PW Whitfield, and KK Hammerstrom (2002). "Analysis of seagrass recovery in experimental excavations and propeller-scar disturbances in the Florida Keys National Marine Sanctuary". *Journal of Coastal Research*. 37:75-85.

Key West Chamber of Commerce, 2002, 1999. http://www.keywestchamber.org/cominfo/demo_economy.htm

Lapointe, BE (1992). "Final Report: Eutrophication and Trophic Structuring of Marine Plant Communities in the Florida Keys". Prepared for Monroe County and Florida Department of Environmental Regulation. Reproduced by U. S. Department of Commerce, National Technical Information Service. Springfield, Virginia.

Lee, ZP, MR Zhang, KL Carder, and LO Hall (1998). "A neural network approach to deriving optical properties and depths of shallow waters". In *Proceedings of SPIE (Ocean Optics XIV)*. Palos Verdes Estates, CA: SPIE.

Leeworthy, V and P Vanasse (1999). "Economic Contribution of Recreating Visitors to the Florida Keys / Key West: Updates for Years 1996-97 and 1997-98". National Oceanic and Atmospheric Administration.

Lewis, RR (1987). "The restoration and creation of seagrass meadows in the southeast United States". *FL. Mar. Res. Publ.* 42:153-73.

Lott, C (1996). <u>Site Characterization for the Florida Keys National Marine Sanctuary and Environs</u>. Vol. 7: Nekton, Plankton, and Oceanic Influences. The Nature Conservancy, Florida and Caribbean Marine Conservation Science Center-University of Miami.

Monroe County Department of Marine Resources (1995). "Inventory of Marinas and Boat Ramps."

Monroe County Growth Management (2001). Department of Planning and Environmental Resources. http://www.co monroe fl.us/pages/hottopics/pf/3%20Growth.pdf.

Monroe County Board of Commissioners (1993). "Technical Document – Monroe County Comprehensive Plan." National Oceanic and Atmospheric Administration (NOAA). Center for Coastal Fisheries and Habitat Research. http://shrimp.ccfhrb noaa.gov/lab/labres.html

National Oceanic and Atmospheric Administration (NOAA) (1995a). "Environmental Assessment for the Structural Restoration of the *M/V Alec Owen Maitland* Grounding Site, Key Largo National Marine Sanctuary, Florida". Prepared by Industrial Economics, Inc., Cambridge, MA.

National Oceanic and Atmospheric Administration (NOAA) (1995b) (revised 2000). "Habitat Equivalency Analysis: An Overview". http://www.darp.noaa.gov/pdf/heaoverv.pdf. Damage Assessment Center, National Ocean Service, NOAA. Silver Spring, Maryland.

National Oceanic and Atmospheric Administration (NOAA) (1996a). "*R/V Columbus Iselin* Grounding Lost Use Damages Looe Key Reef, Looe Key National Marine Sanctuary". Prepared by Norman Meade, Damage Assessment Center, NOAA. Silver Spring, Maryland.

National Oceanic and Atmospheric Administration (NOAA) (1996b). "Florida Keys National Marine Sanctuary, Final Management Plan/Environmental Impact Statement". Volume II. NOAA. Silver Spring, Maryland.

National Oceanic and Atmospheric Administration (NOAA) (1997). "A Socioeconomic Analysis of the Recreation Activities of Monroe County Residents in the Florida Keys/Key West". Prepared by VR Leeworthy and PC

Wiley, Strategic Environmental Assessments Division, Office of Ocean Resources Conservation and Assessment, National Ocean Service, NOAA. Silver Spring, Maryland.

National Oceanic and Atmospheric Administration (NOAA) (1998). "Tidal Bench Marks, Florida". http://www.opsd.nos.noaa.gov/bench/fl/. Accessed 19 August, 1999.

National Oceanic and Atmospheric Administration (NOAA) (2002). "Environmental Assessment: *M/V Wellwood* Grounding Site Restoration". NOAA. Silver Spring, Maryland.

National Weather Service (NWS) (1994). "Hurricanes...Unleashing Nature's Fury". U.S. Department of Commerce, National Oceanic and Atmospheric Administration, NWS, Silver Spring, Maryland. www nws.noaa.gov/om/hurrbro htm. Dated March, 1994; Accessed August 20, 1999.

Peterson BJ and JW Fourqurean (2001). "Large-scale patterns in seagrass (*Thalassia testudinum*) demographics in south Florida". *Limnology andOceanography* 46:1077-90.

Phillips, RC and EG Meñez (1988). "Seagrasses". Smithsonian Contribution to the Marine Sciences, Number 34. Smithsonian Institution Press. Washington, D. C.

Pitts, PA (1994). "An investigation of near-bottom flow patterns along and across Hawk Creek, Florida Keys". *Bulletin of Marine Science* 54(3):610-20.

Powell, GVN, WJ Kenworthy, and JW Fourqurean (1989). "Experimental evidence for nutrient limitation of seagrass growth in a tropical estuary with restricted circulation". *Bulletin of Marine Science* 44(1):35-48.

Sargent, FJ, TJ Leary, DW Crewz, and CR Kruer (1995). "Scarring of Florida's seagrasses: Assessment and Management Options". Florida Marine Research Institute Technical Report TR-1.

Schomer, NS and RD Drew (1982). "An Ecological Characterization of the Lower Everglades, Florida Bay and the Florida Keys". FWS/OBS-82/58.1. U.S. Fish and Wildlife Service, Office of Biological Services, Washington, DC.

Sheridan, P, G McMahan, G Conley, A Williams, and G Thayer (1997). "Nekton Use of Macrophyte Patches Following Mortality of Turtlegrass, *Thalassia testudinum* in Shallow Waters of Florida Bay (Florida, USA)". *Bulletin of Marine Science* 61(3):80120.

Smith, NP (1994). "Long-term Gulf-to-Atlantic transport through tidal channels in the Florida Keys". *Bulletin of Marine Science* 54(3):602-9.

Terrell, B (1994). Fathoming our Past: Historical Contexts of the National Marine Sanctuaries, National Oceanic and Atmospheric Administration and The Mariners' Museum.

Thayer, GW, WF Hettler, Jr., AJ Chester, DR Colby, and PJ McElhaney (1987). "Distribution and Abundance of Fish Communities Among Selected Estuarine and Marine Habitats in Everglades National Park". South Florida Research Center Report, SFRC-87/02. U. S. Department of Commerce, National Marine Fisheries Service, National Oceanic and Atmospheric Administration, Southeast Fisheries Center, Beaufort Laboratory, Beaufort, North Carolina.

Tomasko, D and BE Lapointe (1991). "Productivity and biomass of *Thalassia testudinum* as related to water column nutrient availability and epiphyte levels: Field observations and experimental studies". *Marine Ecology Progress Series* 75:9-17.

United Nations Environment Programme and International Union for the Conservation of Nature (UNEP/IUCN) (1988). Coral Reefs of the World. 3 vols. United Nations Environment Programme and International Union for the Conservation of Nature, Nairobi, Switzerland, and Cambridge, UK.

United States Department of Commerce Economics and Statistics Administration, Bureau of Economic Analysis (USDOC) (1998). "REIS - Regional Economic Information System 1969-96" (CD-ROM). U. S. Department of Commerce, Economics and Statistics Administration, Bureau of Economic Analysis, Washington, DC.

United States Environmental Protection Agency (USEPA) (1999a). "Aerometric Information Retrieval System (AIRS)". http://www.epa.gov/airsdata/. Accessed August 23, 1999.

United States Environmental Protection Agency (USEPA) (1999b). "EnviroFacts Database". http://www.epa.gov/envirofw/html/database html. Accessed August 20, 1999.

United States Fish and Wildlife Service (2004). "Threatened and Endangered Species System (TESS)". Available at http://ecos fws.gov/tess_public/TESSSpeciesReport. Accessed on July 23, 2004.

Whitfield PW, WJ Kenworthy, KK Hammerstrom, and MS Fonseca (2002). "The role of a hurricane in the expansion of disturbances initiated by motor vessels on seagrass banks". *Journal of Coastal Research*: 37:86-99.

Williams, SL (1990). Experimental Studies of Caribbean Seagrass bed Development. *Ecol. Monog.* 60:449-69.

Worm, B, TBH Reusch, HK Lotze (2000). "In Situ Nutrient Enrichment: Methods for Marine Benthic Ecology". *International Review of Hydrobiology*. 85:359-75.

Zieman, JC (1982). "The Ecology of the Seagrasses of South Florida: A Community Profile". U. S. Fish and Wildlife Services, Office of Biological Services, FWS/OBS-82/25. Washington, D. C.

Zieman, JC, and RT Zieman (1989). "The Ecology of the Seagrass Meadows of the West Coast of Florida: A Community Profile". U. S. Fish and Wildlife Services, Biological Report 85(7.25). Washington, D. C.

Zieman, JC (1998). United States v. Great Lakes Dredge and Dock Co., et al Civil Action No. 97-2510-Civ-Davis. Report submitted by: Dr. Joseph C Zieman. Prepared for U.S. Department of Commerce, National Oceanic and Atmospheric Administration, National Ocean Service, Office of Ocean and Coastal Resource Management, Marine Sanctuaries Division. Silver Spring, Maryland.

APPENDIX A: EXAMPLE ORPHAN INJURY ASSESSMENT AND MONITORING SUMMARY FOR THE SEAGRASS REGIONAL RESTORATION PLAN

NAME OF INJURY SITE: *EXAMPLE*
REGION: MIDDLE KEYS

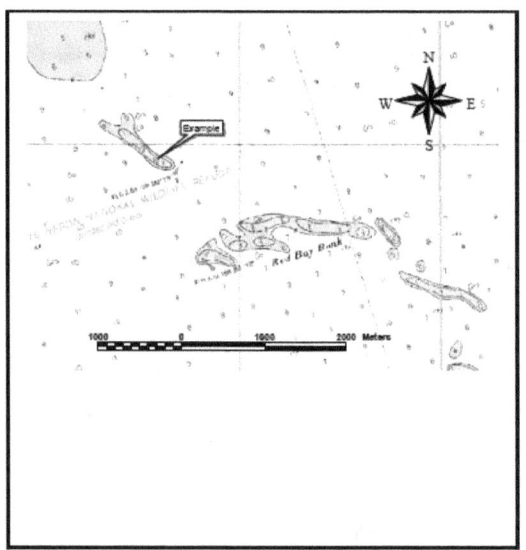

Figure A-1: *Example* Injury Site Location

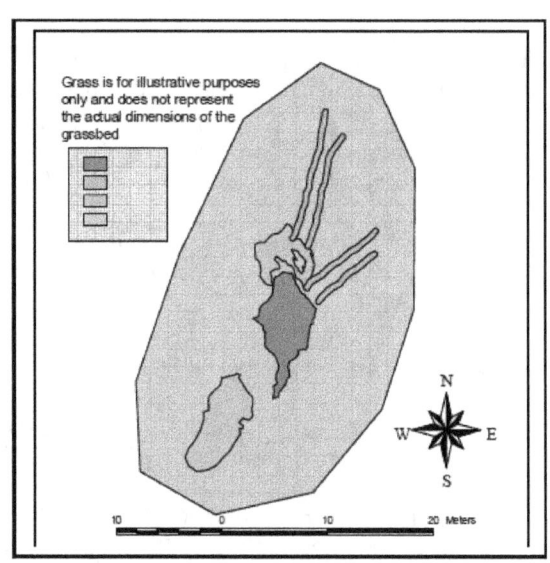

Figure A-2: Physical Dimensions of Injury

A.1   INJURY DESCRIPTION

Location of Injury: Bayside Moser Channel near marker 13 (Marathon, FL)

Lat/Long Position: N 024° 45.8941' W 081° 10.5936' (blowhole)
                                         N 024° 45.9038' W 081° 10.5908' (North-South propscars)
                                         N 024° 45.8982' W 081° 10.5885' (Northeast-Southwest propscars)

Substrate Type: Primarily *Halimeda* spp. hash, coral rubble, and carbonate sands and muds

Table A-1: Site Characteristics

Site Characteristic	Disturbance Level (1-5, 5 is Highest)	Comments
Orientation (relative to main flow axis)		
Flow Magnitude/Current Speed		
Wave Exposure		
Sediment Particle Size		
Drift Algae or Litter Accumulation in Injury Site		
Instantaneous or Historical Characterization (1 or 0)		

Table A-2: Injury Dimensions

	AREA (m2)	LENGTH (m)	WIDTH (m)	DIRECTION	DEPTH (m)	VOLUME (m3)
Blowhole 1	30.7	NA*	NA	NA	.9	13.27
Propscar 1	6.17	11.64	.53	North-South	NA	Na
Propscar 2	5.5	10.38	.53	North-South	NA	NA
Propscar 3	4.58	8.32	.55	SW-NE	NA	NA
Propscar 4	3.78	6.88	.55	SW-NE	NA	NA
Berm	45.06	NA	NA	NA	NA	NA

*NA=Not Applicable

Table A-3: Percent Cover of Seagrass Species

	Species	Inside Injury	Surrounding Habitat
Percent Cover	T. testudinum	1.00%	19.00%
	H. wrightii	0.00%	0.00%
	S. filiforme	0.00%	1.00%
	Total		20.00%

Figure A-3: Bathymetry of *Example* Injury

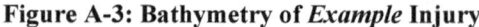

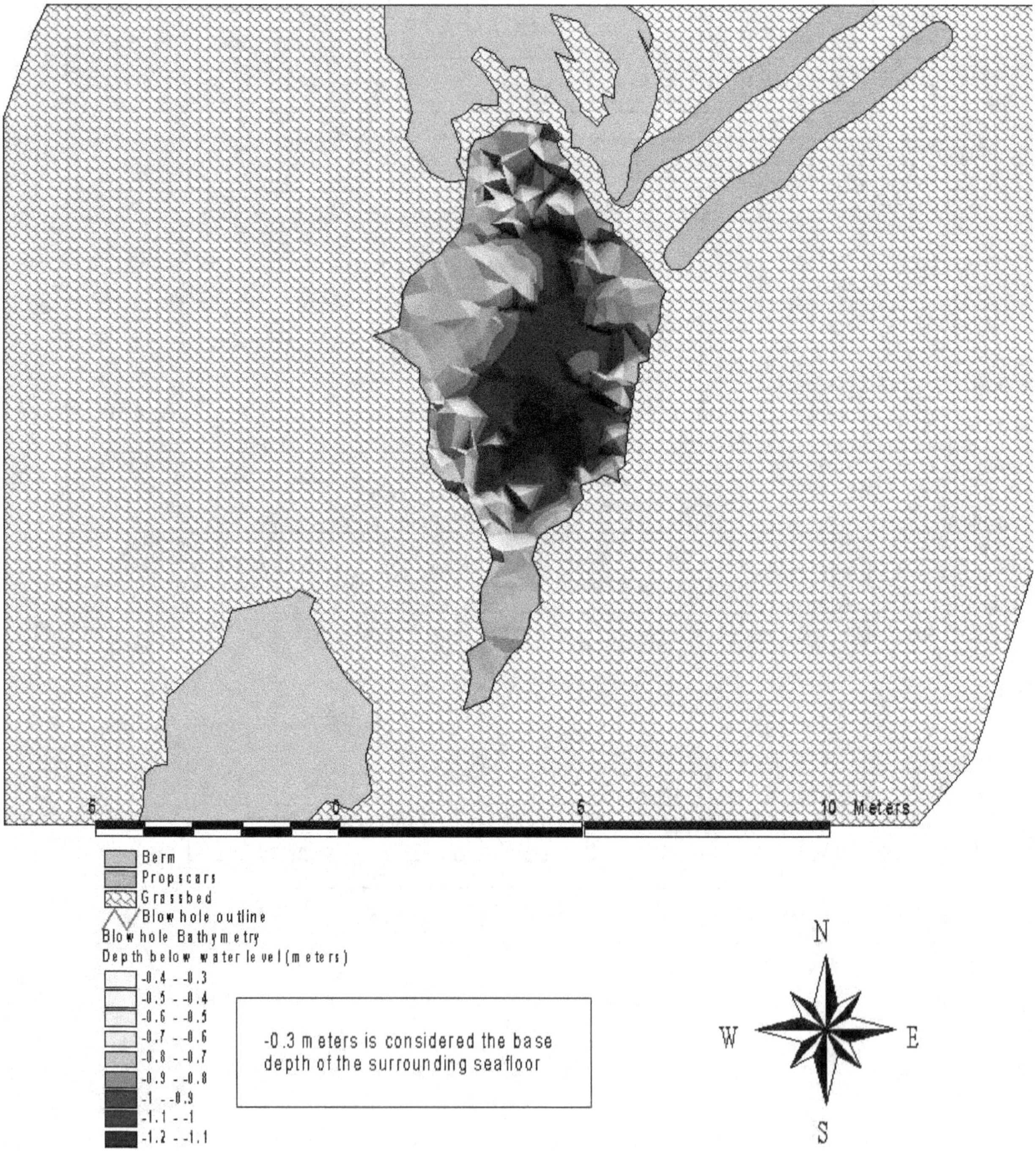
5
0
5
10 Meters
Berm
Propscars
Grassbed
Blowhole outline
Blowhole Bathymetry
Depth below water level (meters)
-0.4 - -0.3
-0.5 - -0.4
-0.6 - -0.5
-0.7 - -0.6
-0.8 - -0.7
-0.9 - -0.8
-1 - -0.9
-1.1 - -1
-1.2 - -1.1
-0.3 meters is considered the base depth of the surrounding seafloor
N
W
E
S

A.2   PROPOSED RESTORATION ACTIONS

a)   Bird Stakes. The grounding site requires a total of 74 stakes (see Figure A-4).

b)   Seagrass Transplants. The grounding site requires a total of 83 seagrass-planting units (*S. filiforme*) (see Figure A-4).

c)   Sediment Fill. The grounding site requires a total of 13.27 cubic meters of sediment fill prior to staking and planting.

Figure A-4: Staking and Planting of *Example* Orphan Injury Site

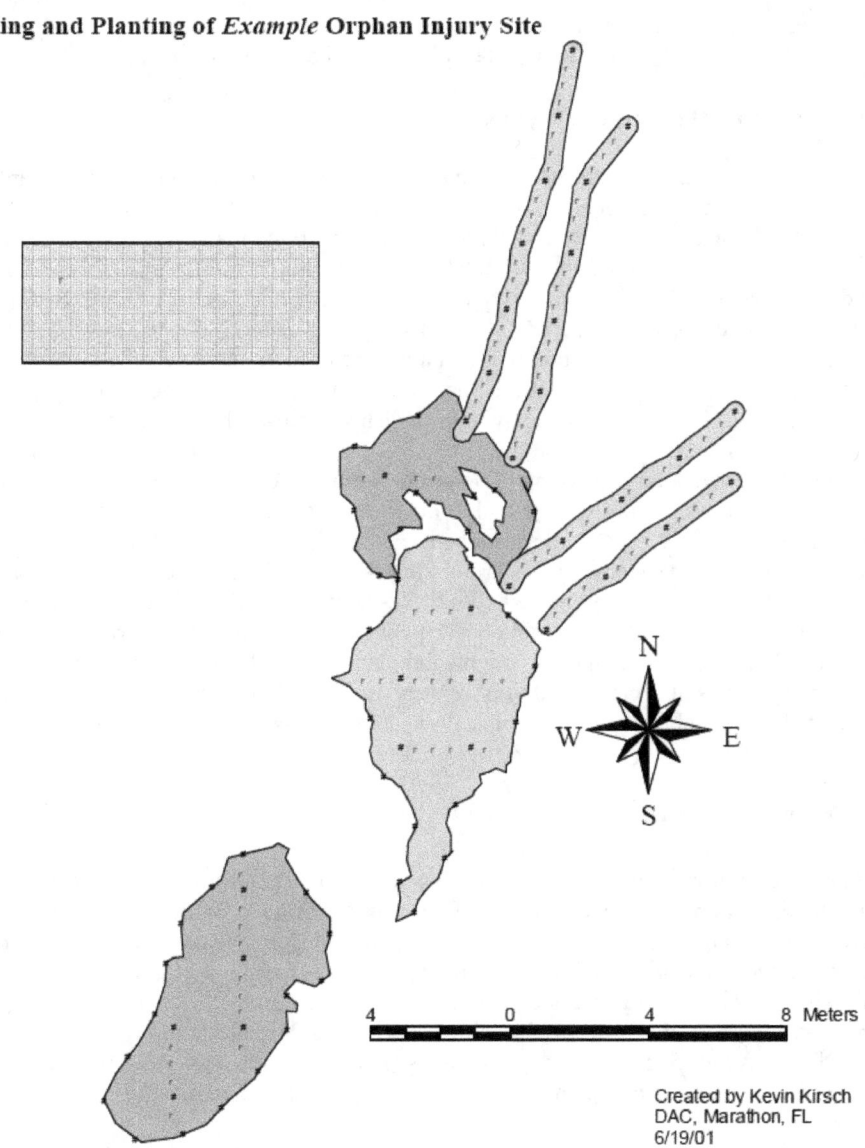

Created by Kevin Kirsch
DAC, Marathon, FL
6/19/01

A.3   MONITORING

A.3.1   Site Identification

The grounding injury can be re-located by future monitoring teams by referencing the documented differential global positioning system coordinates.

A.3.2   Monitoring Variables

The following monitoring parameters will be observed and/or measured at the site(s):
1) initial survival of seagrass transplants;
2) incidence of seagrass re-colonization from transplants and or the undisturbed side populations by percent area covered; and
3) structural integrity of the bird stakes, planting units, and/or sediment fill.

A.3.3   Monitoring Data Processing and Utility

Monitoring events will assess transplant and natural re-colonization via measures of planting unit (PU) survival, areal coverage, and documentation with video transects. The execution and application of the monitoring effort is adapted from "Guidelines for the Conservation and Restoration of Seagrasses in the United States and Adjacent Waters", available at: http://shrimp.bea.nmfs.gov/library/digital html - under "Appendices" - pages 207-220, or http://www.cop.noaa.gov/pubs/das/das12.html. Briefly, the monitoring data will be used to determine if successful establishment of planted seagrass has occurred and if it is on an appropriate recovery trajectory. If not, these data will be used to plan and execute remedial restoration. The success criteria are: 1) whether planted material has a minimum of one rhizome apical per PU, a PU survival rate 75% of the planting units having established themselves by the end of Year 1. If it is determined that less than 75% survival has occurred by the end of Year 1, then remedial planting should occur during the next available planting period to bring the percentage survival rate to the minimum standard by the next monitoring survey, and 3) the measured growth rate of bottom coverage from either direct quadrat surveys or video-based assessment (p. 220 above; Braun-Blanquet assessment). The growth rate should be considered successful if, starting after one year, the planted, pioneering species of seagrass in the scars (restoration sites) is projected with 95% statistical confidence, to achieve complete bottom coverage (with pre-injury levels of shoot density) within the five year monitoring period for original plantings. If this criterion is not met, then remedial planting should occur during the next available planting period. Videotaping is also performed to provide an unambiguous record of the status of the restoration that is particularly valuable to parties not familiar with seagrass systems and interpretation of statistical data.

A.3.4   Monitoring Schedule

The primary restoration-monitoring plan developed for this site requires a principal and assistant biologist to complete eight monitoring events over a five-year period (see Table A-4). During the first year, two monitoring events are scheduled at intervals of 180 and 360 days. Two monitoring events are also conducted the second year. Monitoring events will assess transplant and natural re-colonization survival, shoot density, aerial coverage, and documentation with video transects. As conditions at the restoration site are subject to change from storms or climatic events, one additional monitoring event is scheduled per year for years three through five (at 180 days) to assess restoration recovery, and if necessary, to conduct mid-course corrections (e.g., replanting of seagrass, insertion of stakes, etc.).

Each monitoring event will consist of two biologists working approximately two days per monitoring event. The number of days per monitoring event reflects travel time and the possibility of inclement weather that may necessitate multiple visits to the site. Two biologists are necessary for safety as well as for reducing the potential for errors in measurements, plantings, and observations. Following each field trip, up to one day will be required to process the observations and measurements, enter information into a database, analyze the data, and prepare a report. Also included in this period is the time necessary to transcribe field notes, develop film, and identify and record all photographic slides and/or videotapes.

Table A-4. Categories and Timing of Primary Monitoring

		Survival Monitoring	Braun Blanquet Abundance	Video Transects
Year 1	60 days	X		X
	180 days	X	X	X
	360 days	X	X	X
Year 2	180 days		X	X
	360 days		X	X
Year 3	180 days		X	X
Year 4	180 days		X	X
Year 5	180 days		X	X
Number of PUs sampled		Every PU	Scars: Every PU; Holes/Berms: Minimum of 10% of PUs	Scars: Every PU; Blowholes/Berms: 5 randomly selected rows (all if <5 rows)

* PU=Planting Unit

A.4   ESTIMATED COST OF ORPHAN SITE RESTORATION

Prior to implementing restoration at the selected orphan injury site, the estimated cost of restoration, monitoring, and oversight will be calculated. This will be done to ensure that sufficient compensatory funds have been collected and pooled from NRDA cases to complete the project, once started. The estimated restoration costs for the example site are (in 2004 dollars):

Restoration Costs	$16,403
Restoration Monitoring Costs	$4,784
Restoration Oversight Costs	$3,221
Subtotal NOAA Restoration Costs	**$24,408**

APPENDIX B. COMMENTS RECEIVED ON THE DRAFT PROGRAMMATIC ENVIRONMENTAL IMPACT STATEMENT FOR SEAGRASS RESTORATION AND RESPONSES TO COMMENTS

Four written comments were received on the DPEIS during the public comment period that was open from June 25, 2004 through August 9, 2004. The comments were received from:

1. Heinz J. Mueller, NEPA Program Office Chief, Office of Policy and Management, Region 4, United States Environmental Protection Agency
2. Pat Wells, Park Manager, Lignumvitae Key Botanical State Park, Florida Department of Environmental Protection
3. Miles M. Croom, Assistant Regional Administrator, Habitat Conservation Division, Region 4, United States Environmental Protection Agency
4. Roy R. "Robin" Lewis, III, Professional Wetland Scientist and Certified Senior Ecologist with The Ecological Society of America.

These comments and the Trustees' responses to the comments are included in this appendix.

B.1 COMMENT RECEIVED FROM HEINZ J. MUELLER, EPA

The following six-page comment was received from Heinz J. Mueller, NEPA Program Office Chief, Office of Policy and Management, Region 4, United States Environmental Protection Agency on July 15, 2004.

This space intentionally left blank.

UNITED STATES ENVIRONMENTAL PROTECTION AGENCY
REGION 4
ATLANTA FEDERAL CENTER
61 FORSYTH STREET
ATLANTA, GEORGIA 30303-8960

July 13, 2004

Ms. Harriet Sopher
National Marine Sanctuary Program
1305 East-West Highway
N/ORM4 Station 11653
Silver Spring, MD 20910

SUBJ: EPA Review of the NOAA "Draft Programmatic Environmental Impact Statement [DPEIS] for Seagrass Restoration in the Florida Keys National Marine Sanctuary [FKNMS]"; Monroe County, Florida

Dear Ms. Sopher:

The U.S. Environmental Protection Agency (EPA) has reviewed the referenced National Oceanic and Atmospheric Administration (NOAA) DPEIS in accordance with our responsibilities under Section 102(2)(C) of the National Environmental Policy Act (NEPA) and Section 309 of the Clean Air Act. The subject DPEIS, which was prepared in consultation with the Florida Department of Environmental Protection (FDEP), programmatically presents several alternatives to restore seagrasses damaged by boat groundings (propeller scars, blowholes and sediment berms) in FKNMS waters. Overall, EPA fully supports the restoration goals due to the numerous seagrass scarrings within FKNMS, the ecological value of seagrasses (water quality, habitat, fisheries nursery, sediment stabilizer and shoreline buffer), and the "living laboratory" uniqueness of the Sanctuary. Local seagrass species to be restored are turtle grass (*Thalassia testudinum*), manatee grass (*Syringodium filiforme*), and shoal grass (*Halodule wrightii*), with turtle grass being the dominant species within FKNMS.

The restoration alternatives proposed by NOAA include: 1) no action, 2) seagrass transplants, 3) bird stakes, 4) fertilizer stakes, 5) sediment fill, 6) sediment tubes, 7) berm redistribution, 8) sod replacement, 9) water markers, and 10) exclusion cages. These options would be used singularly or in combinations, with additional options also being possible. More specifically, these alternatives would restore grassbeds through natural revegetation (no action); seagrass sprigging from nearby donor sites (seagrass transplants); natural fertilization of scarred areas in shallow waters (bird stakes); artificial fertilization of scarred areas in deeper waters (fertilizer stakes); state- and federally-permitted refilling of blowholes with new sediment (sediment fill); refilling of scarred and erosional (high energy) areas with meshed substrate (sediment tubes); grading of bermed areas to pre-grounding levels through manual raking or water-hosing (berm redistribution); replanting of intact seagrass plugs (sod replacement); placement of water markers to signal shallow, vulnerable seagrass beds to boaters (water markers); and placement of cages over restored grassbeds near coral reefs to prevent overgrazing by reef herbivores (exclusion cages). While some of these options would produce minor environmental impacts (e.g., turbidity, air quality, noise, etc.), the overall effects of successful

73

seagrass restoration would be beneficial to the environment of the Sanctuary.

Although EPA supports the goals of the proposed effort, we offer the following comments and suggestions for NOAA's consideration in the development of the Final PEIS (FPEIS):

▸ **NEPA Process**

* *Preferred Alternative* - Although NEPA does not require identification of a preferred alternative in draft NEPA documents, it is desirable from a public standpoint. That is, identification of a preferred alternative by the federal lead agency will allow the public to focus on the alternative that the lead agency will likely select in its final document and/or Record of Decision (ROD), as well as implement in the field. In the case of an overarching NEPA document such as a PEIS, selection of a preferred alternative is somewhat difficult. If a preferred restoration alternative (or a hybrid alternative) cannot reasonably be selected for the FPEIS or even the ROD, we suggest that for the purposes of NEPA, the FPEIS be somewhat reconfigured to indicate a clear commitment to overall seagrass restoration (which would become the preferred alternative) and compare such action to no restoration (no action). The specific restoration alternatives considered in the DPEIS would then become subalternatives or options of restoration and would be selected on a case-by-case basis in the presumed future site-specific restoration documents that would tier from the PEIS.

* *Tiering* - As a PEIS, we assume there will be some site-specific NEPA documents that will tier from the PEIS (Environmental Assessments (EAs) or possibly Categorical Exclusions (CEs)). The FPEIS should discuss this in terms of what thresholds would be used to generate such a document. In addition, we also suggest that the FPEIS better relate restoration alternatives to the field (specific regions of the Sanctuary) by reasonably predicting which scarred areas within the FKNMS might require site-specific NEPA documentation. If possible, candidate restoration alternatives should be identified for these regions. For example, the general areas for the use of the exclusion cage alternative could presumably be relatively easily located since it would only be used near coral reefs to restrict reef herbivores (we also note that the restoration plan in Appendix J provides some site-specific information). However, if defining such general use areas is too specific at this time, perhaps the percentage of application for each alternative could be estimated (e.g., it is expected that some 20% of the scarred areas would be restored through sediment filling in combination with seagrass transplanting).

* *Other Alternatives* - The DPEIS (pg. 50) indicates that other alternatives not detailed in the DPEIS may also be used as methods of restoration. The document also indicates (pg. 5) that addendums to the PEIS could be possible. We suggest that all feasible alternatives be identified in the FPEIS with their impacts documented. Details and final designs of selected options could subsequently be addressed in the site-specific documents as necessary, thereby avoiding the need for addendums to the PEIS. However, the alternatives considered in the PEIS should be broad enough to bracket all likely site-specific alternatives. Field adaptive management modifications could also be made if methodologies remain within these brackets.

▸ **Other General Comments**

  * *Seagrass Transplants* - Although various restoration alternatives are offered, actual transplanting (as opposed to natural revegetation) seems essential to overall restoration to ensure and expedite the process. However, it is our understanding that seagrass transplanting is historically difficult and often unsuccessful. The FPEIS should discuss the success rates of seagrass transplants for all three species, referencing specific NOAA or other recent studies from the literature. Also, what criteria would be used to determine successful restoration (e.g., % cover, % survival, growth/biomass/colonization; flowering/reproduction; etc.). Will monitoring be applied to ensure such success and initiate follow-up as needed?

  * *Bird Stakes* - Page 7 indicates that bird stakes with roosting blocks may have the disadvantage of being confused (by boaters) as water markers or navigational aids. This could be a significant consequence since it could result is additional groundings and propeller scarring and thereby be counterproductive to the restoration effort. We therefore suggest that bird stakes be made to appear more distinct from navigational markers (e.g., colored, striped or otherwise distinctively marked PVC posts). This change in color pattern should also be incorporated into the boater education program.

Also related to bird stakes, it is unclear from the DPEIS (pg. 33) if such an approach would substantively affect local water quality in Sanctuary areas that are not well flushed. Unless the bird droppings fall to the seafloor and the nutrients remain close to the stake rather than disperse locally, phytoplankton blooms could occur in adjacent, low-energy areas. Such blooms could affect light penetration and thereby retard seagrass growth and survival. We suggest monitoring where appropriate to verify nutrient proximity near the stake, as well as further discussion in the FPEIS with references cited.

  * *Sediment Fill* - The FPEIS (pg. 9) indicates that 0.25-inch pea gravel would be used as sediment fill. While we agree that such grain size would provide needed weight to resist normal wave action, it is unclear if seagrass rhizomes would thrive in such substrate. However, we assume that fines from the area would eventually fill the interstitial spaces of the pea gravel to allow successful seagrass anchoring and growth.

  * *No Action* - The no action alternative would depend on natural revegetation. In addition to this process being slower and less reliable than active restoration techniques, it may be noted that natural revegetation could also allow the colonization of undesirable, opportunistic (invasive) species such as blue-green algae to revegetate the scarred areas and become established, as opposed to the desired seagrass species.

  * *Water Markers* - The use of water markers to signal shallow water or seagrass meadows is certainly beneficial to the FKNMS. This alternative, however, is a preventative measure rather than a restoration alternative. While EPA supports preventative measures, this option seems out of place in the list of restoration alternatives. Instead, we suggest that a section on methods to prevent seagrass injury be included in the FPEIS. This section would help educate the public (and reduce the need for future restorations) and could include the information on water markers as well as other preventative measures.

* *Monitoring* - The success of some of the proposed restoration alternatives are time sensitive. That is, in order for the berm redistribution option to save covered seagrasses underlying the sediment berm (i.e., displaced fill created from propeller washings during the salvage of grounded boats), the scar and berm area would need to be identified quickly and the berm redistributed in the scarred area. Other restoration actions should also be timely such as the filling of a scarred area with new sediment so that erosion of the propeller scar does not continue. Similarly, the replanting of displaced sod pieces (due to propeller groundings) must also be accomplished quickly in order to ensure sod re-establishment. Is the continuous monitoring and rapid implementation needed for these actions planned as part of the restoration process?

* *Purpose & Need* - Will this proposal strictly deal with restoration or will any other unvegetated (but not scarred) sandy areas within the Sanctuary be targets for seagrass transplants? We note that a considerable amount of benthic area in the Keys are labeled as "unknown bottoms" in Figure 3-1. These areas might be candidate sites for new grassbeds to provide habitat or attenuate storm surge.

* *Air Quality* - The air quality section (pg. 17) could be updated to include that the ozone 8-hour standard (National Ambient Air Quality Standards: NAAQS) has recently been promulgated by EPA and replaces the 1-hour standard. Monroe County and all of Florida in general is in attainment for the new standard. The PM2.5 (Particulate Matter for air particles 2.5 microns and less in size) standard was also promulgated and all Florida counties are in attainment. Monroe County is also in attainment for all of the other NAAQS criteria pollutants. Also, related to air quality, all project equipment should be tuned to manufacturer's specifications to minimize air (and noise) emissions, although air quality (and noise) impacts from vessels and equipment should be relatively minor overall.

* *Cultural Resources* - We strongly concur with the statement (pg. 28) that "[r]estoration contractors under the supervision of NOAA and/or State personnel will be instructed to halt all activities if cultural resources are discovered until authorization to continue is granted by State and federal cultural resource authorities." We will primarily defer to the State Historic Preservation Officer (SHPO) regarding such authorizations.

* *Marine Debris* - The FPEIS should further discuss the long-termed fate of potential marine debris associated with the exclusion cages alternative (cages) and the sediment tube alternative (anchoring pins and sediment mesh), should these materials become dislodged or vandalized and become floating or benthic marine debris.

76

* *Cumulative Impacts* - Although the introduction to this section (pg. 47) is an excellent summary, the actual cumulative effects discussion by alternative could be improved for the FPEIS. Addressing cumulative impacts for a restoration project is particularly difficult since overall restoration impacts are positive rather than negative. However, one negative cumulative impact that may arise due to this study is the effect of transplants on donor sites. While we note (pg. 31) that donor sites will be "routinely monitored" to prevent source stock degradation, we believe that if monitoring detects cumulative impacts at a donor site, transplants must stop and the site abandoned to maintain the health and viability of the donor site. The FPEIS should further address (pg. 47) how collection of source stock for transplants will not be allowed to degrade healthy donor sites and what threshold would be used to determine donor site cumulative impacts. In addition to potential donor site cumulative effects, public use impacts within the FKNMS could also cumulatively impact the resources of the Sanctuary. Conversely, positive cumulative impacts might also be noted, i.e., the continued erosion/turbidity associated with propeller scars would – once restored – would no longer cumulatively affect other sources of erosion/turbidity in the Sanctuary.

Additional cumulative effects can be assumed if the project area is broadened from only the FKNMS to include projects outside the Sanctuary. For such a larger project area, the minor impacts of the restoration alternatives (e.g., turbidity, air emissions, and noise impacts) could collectively affect the region in association with any nearby projects (e.g., dredging projects in the Keys). Also, any other restorations or mitigative measures being implemented in the region, together with the present seagrass restoration, would collectively provide a greater overall restoration for the Keys and could be referenced in the FPEIS (e.g., education programs, better sewage centralization and treatment, permit conditions, fishing restrictions, anchoring/mooring restrictions, etc.).

* *Editorial Comments* - For your information, we offer the following editorial comments:

+ NRDA (pg. 4) - The acronym "NRDA" was not defined at first mention. In addition to defining acronyms in the text at first mention, we suggest that a List of Acronyms for this and other acronyms in th document be included in the FPEIS.
+ Citation (pg. 10) - The citation "Fonseca et-al 1994" should read "Fonseca et al. 1994".
+ Citation (pg. 16) - The citation "Forquorean et al. 2001" should read "Fourqurean et al. 2001". It should also be noted that this reference is dated since several long-termed monitoring stations are demonstrating eutrophication impacts on seagrasses.
+ Table 3-1 (pg. 16) - For clarity, the column heading of *Benthic Communities* might be modified to read *Vegetative Benthic Communities*.
+ Seagrass Functions (pg. 20) - The fourth seagrass function listed ("shoots retard or slowing currents, by enhancing sediment stability...") should read ("shoots retard or slow currents, thereby enhancing sediment stability...").
+ *Porites furcata* (pg. 20) - The referenced species of *Porites* coral should be

77

verified (*Porites porites?*).

+ Fish List (pg. 21) - The common name for the fish family Bothidae should be changed from "flunder" to "flounder". Similarly, the common name for the family Ephippidae should be changed from "Padefishes" to "Spadefishes".

+ Table 3-4 (pg. 22) - This list of endangered and threatened species should indicate whether the listed species are federally protected and/or state protected. Also, we do not generally associate the osprey as threatened or endangered, but are aware that there are areas where it has been listed. Its status for Monroe County should be verified.

* *EPA Rating* - EPA rates this DPEIS as "LO" (Lack of Objections) in support of the implementation of the restoration alternatives. However, we have some general suggestions as noted above.

* *Summary* - Overall, EPA fully supports the proposed restoration goals for seagrass damage in FKNMS waters. From a NEPA perspective, however, we suggest that additional discussion be provided in the FPEIS on 1) preferred alternatives (i.e., either a commitment to overall restoration or selection of a specific restoration alternative or hybrid), 2) reasonably relating the restoration alternatives to specific regions within the Sanctuary, and 3) defining the thresholds for implementing presumed future site-specific NEPA documents that would tier from the PEIS. The FPEIS should also reference studies on the relative success of seagrass transplants for the selected turtle, manatee and shoal grasses, and also indicate how successful restoration would be defined for the project. The cumulative impacts discussion should also be modified to include assessment of donor site impacts. Monitoring should also be further addressed as it pertains to determining the need for any adaptive management modifications, ensuring successful overall restoration or specific restoration options, donor site impacts, and allowing for early identification of new scarring injuries to grassbeds.

Should you have questions regarding our comments, feel free to contact Chris Hoberg (Atlanta: 404/562-9619) of my staff for NEPA issues or Dr. Bill Kruczynski (Marathon Key, FL: 305/743-0537) of the EPA Water Management Division for seagrass technical issues.

Sincerely,

Heinz Mueller

Heinz J. Mueller, Chief
NEPA Program Office
Office of Policy and Management

cc: Susan Kennedy - NOAA: Silver Spring, MD
       Anne McCarthy - FDEP: Key West, FL

B.2 RESPONSE TO HEINZ J. MUELLER COMMENT

The EPA provides several helpful recommendations. Unless otherwise discussed below, the FPEIS was revised to incorporate all comments.

I.   Bird Stakes

The EPA suggests that the bird stakes be made to appear more distinct from navigational markers by striping or coloring, and incorporating the distinctive bird stake pattern into boater education programs. This suggestion was not included in the FPEIS. To be effective, such a distinctive color pattern must be recognized and understood by boaters. As NOAA currently has limited ability to influence or augment boater education programs in Florida, it is unlikely the meaning of the color pattern could be widely disseminated. In addition, the funds and employee time that would go into coloring the stakes could likely be better spent on other injur\y prevention projects.

II.   Sediment Fill

The EPA states that it is unclear if seagrass rhizomes would thrive in 0.25-inch pea gravel. Currently, there are no published, peer-reviewed sources to document such successful colonization. However, NOAA biologists have conducted extensive experiments on the sediment fill technique, and it has been demonstrated that seagrass transplants will survive in 0.25-inch pea gravel. The results of these experiments are presently being prepared for submission for peer-reviewed publication.

II.   Monitoring

In reference to berm redistribution, sediment fill, and sod replacement restoration actions, the EPA asks "is the continuous monitoring and rapid implementation needed for these actions planned as part of the restoration process?". Following notification of a grounding incident by Florida Fish and Wildlife Conservation Commission officers, restoration biologists conduct injury assessments as soon as weather permits. Sod replacement is done while the biologists are on-scene, immediately following the completion of the injury assessment. If the biologists have the tools necessary to undertake berm redistribution, it is done at the same time. If berm redistribution requires additional outside expertise or equipment (for larger/deeper berms), such action is not currently undertaken until after settlement is reached. NOAA does not have the funds to support such actions prior to settlement. Similarly, sediment fill is only employed after settlement is reached because of funding limitations. NOAA is currently exploring sources of funding to conduct pre-settlement, emergency restoration.

III.   Purpose and Need

The EPA asks if this program will strictly focus on restoration or if any other unvegetated, unimpacted sandy areas within the FKNMS will be targeted for seagrass transplants. This program is designed solely to restore injuries to seagrass habitat that result from vessel groundings.

IV.   Editorial Comments

The acronym "NRDA" is first used and defined on page 1 of the DPEIS. A list of acronyms was added in the FPEIS. The "Benthic Communities" section heading was retained because not all communities discussed in the section were "Vegetative Benthic Communities".

B.3 COMMENT RECEIVED FROM PAT WELLS, FDEP

The following one-page comment was received from Pat Wells, Park Manager, Lignumvitae Key Botanical State Park, Florida Department of Environmental Protection on August 2, 2004.

3.9.4 Endangered and Threatened Species

This section needs to be redone. Characterizing marine turtles and mammals as seasonal visitors is incorrect. Bottle nosed dolphins and marine turtles, for some populations and age classes, are year round residents to the Florida Keys. FWC's, Fish and Wildlife Research Institute have staff with the data and expertise to rewrite this section.

3.10 Cultural Resources

3.10.1 Background

"The Seminoles were the predominant Native American group in the area before complete Euro-American settlement." This statement is probably correct for the late 1700's and 1800's but totally ignores the original aboriginal inhabitants, like the Tequesta and Calusa. These cultures and their ancestry are the true natives to this area and were the mound builders. If submerged cultures resources are present, they would of come these cultures not the Seminoles. Section 3.10.2 presents this more accurately.

4.2.4 Biological Resources (No Action Alternative)

Direct Effects

Paragraph two: Again the characterizing marine turtles as seasonal migrates. The FKNMS is a developmental habitat for a number of marine turtle species. Immature populations of green turtles depend heavily on seagrass beds as a foraging habitat. The direct effects of the "No Action Alternative" is a prolonged lose of a finite habitat thus has the potential of negatively effecting endangered and threatened species dependent on the habitat.

B.4 RESPONSE TO PAT WELLS COMMENT

All comments were incorporated in the FPEIS.

B.5 COMMENT RECEIVED FROM Miles M. Croom, EPA

The following one-page comment was received from Miles M. Croom, Assistant Regional Administrator, Habitat Conservation Division, Region 4, United States Environmental Protection Agency on August 9, 2004.

UNITED STATES DEPARTMENT OF COMMERCE
National Oceanic and Atmospheric Administration
NATIONAL MARINE FISHERIES SERVICE

Southeast Regional Office
9721 Executive Center Drive N
St. Petersburg, Florida 33702
(727) 570-5317, FAX (727) 570-5300
http://sero.nmfs.noaa.gov/

August 9, 2004   F/SER4:DD

MEMORANDUM FOR: Harriet Sopher
                    National Marine Sanctuary Program

FROM: Miles M. Croom
                    Assistant Regional Administrator, Habitat Conservation Division

SUBJECT: Draft Programmatic Environmental Impact Statement for Seagrass
                    Restoration in the Florida Keys National Marine Sanctuary

This responds to the June 25, 2004, Notice of Availability for the subject document. As specified in the Magnuson-Stevens Fishery Conservation and Management Act, EFH consultation is required for Federal actions which may adversely affect EFH. However, as the Federal action agency in this matter, the National Marine Sanctuary Program has determined that the proposed restoration activities would not adversely affect EFH and, based on our review, we agree with your determination. Please be advised that further consultation on this matter is not necessary unless future modifications are proposed and you believe that resulting action may result in adverse impacts to EFH.

cc: PPI/SP - S. Kennedy
        File

B.6 RESPONSE TO MILES M. CROOM COMMENT

This comment requires no changes to be made to the FPEIS.

B.7 COMMENT RECEIVED FROM ROY R. "ROBIN" LEWIS, III

The following seven-page comment was received from Roy R. "Robin" Lewis, III, Professional Wetland Scientist and Certified Senior Ecologist with The Ecological Society of America on July 9, 2004.

This space intentionally left blank

P.O. Box 5430
Salt Springs, FL 32134
July 9, 2004

Harriet Sopher
National Marine Sanctuary Program
1305 East West Highway
N/ORM4 Station 11653
Silver Spring, MD 20910

RE: Draft Programmatic EIS (DPEIS) for Seagrass Restoration in the Florida Keys
National Marine Sanctuary (FKNMS)

Dear Ms. Sopher:

I have reviewed the DPEIS and would provide these comments.

The purpose of the proposed action, as stated on page 1, is to systematically evaluate the
short and long-term environmental and socioeconomic effects of the implementation of
seagrass restoration and injury prevention projects in the FKNMS in general compliance
with NEPA guidance, and specifically NOAA guidance on compliance with NEPA. I
would say upfront that I do not believe the document adequately addresses these issues,
and in particular does not address the issues raised during Scoping by myself (via email
on March 30, 2003) and Pat McNeese (by letter dated April 2, 2003) (see copies of
communications attached).

In particular we both emphasized our experience with these issues in the FKNMS, and
our recommendation that prevention of seagrass damage via better channel marking,
designating areas closed to boating, education, compliance monitoring and enforcement,
were the priorities if the amount of damage were to be decreased in future years. I believe
NOAA guidance on compliance with NEPA requires such issues to be directly addressed.

As a professional biologist with over 30 years experience working in Florida Keys
seagrass and mangrove ecosystems, it is my professional opinion that the document treats
key issues in a very superficial manner, and does not address others at all. There are five
key issues I wish to address, and would point out that most were previously raised in the
Scoping process.

I. Magnitude of the Problem — Cumulative Area of Seagrass Impacted and the Real
Costs of Restoration

The estimate of 60-70% of the reported 677 groundings in the FKNMS in 2001 that may
have occurred in seagrass meadows yields 406 events at the 60% estimate. If one
assumes that each is approximately the size of the example given in Attachment B to
Appendix J (total 95.8 square meters including grounding damage and prop scar
damage), that would total 38,894.8 square meters or 3.89 ha for that year. If one assumes

83

that this level of damage has been occurring since the FKNMS was established in 1990 (which including orphan grounding sites not quantified in the report is a reasonable estimate), a minimum of 54.46 ha of grounding site damage spread over 5,684 sites would have occurred. Using the restoration cost estimate in Attachment B, page 154, of S23,247 (which I estimate is off by 5X or I OX of the real costs), total restoration of these 5,684 sites would require $9,438,282 to have been spent. If one uses the cost estimate in Fonseca et at. (2002) (page 167) of $940,000 per hectare (1996 dollars), the cost would have been $51,192,400 to repair and monitor all these seagrass damage sites.

The above listed numbers and costs are still a conservative estimate of total damage to seagrasses as the 30,000 acres of prop scarring in the Florida Keys documented in Sargent et al. (1995), and based on 1991 aerial photography, appears not to be documented nor discussed as a problem needing to be addressed in the document. What is the status of prop scarring damage in the FKNMS thirteen years later? Has it increased or decreased based upon prevention efforts to date? Again, prevention through better channel marking, education, and enforcement are the answer for the future.

Key questions that must be addressed therefore are: How many grounding sites and major prop scar sites, like Windley Key (Figure 10 in Sargent et al. 1995) have been restored back to reference conditions since the FKNMS was established? Has even a single site been completely restored?? How much did it really cost to do these restorations if done? Are these costs applied anywhere in the document to explain the real magnitude of what is referred to on page 25 as "the dollar value of the restoration actions themselves is low" (without quantification). Anywhere between $9-5I million dollars seems not to be "low." Perhaps related to the construction of a large condo in the Keys it is, but in relation to the total amount of dollars actually collected from both in and out-of-court settlements to get the job done, what does it really represent? How much money has been collected, by whom, and where is it deposited (what agency and what account?). How much has been spent to date on: (a) administration and research and (b) actual physical restoration of grounding sites in the FKNMS? None of this is discussed or even mentioned under socioeconomics or even in Table 2-2, page 12, where seagrass restoration alternatives are listed. Why is the cost of restoration and protection not a factor to be considered?

The reason that listing and discussion of costs are essential, as stated on page 1 of the document, is that "(T)he types of seagrass restoration and injury prevention projects proposed in this plan will be implemented with funds collected through natural resource damage assessment (NRDA) settlements for injuries to seagrasses within the FNMS. The anticipated beneficial and adverse environmental and socioeconomic impacts of each restoration technique will be discussed in detail later in this document" (emphasis added). Specific reference to how the settlement funds are to be spent is referenced on page 52 with a referral to the National Marine Sanctuaries Act (NMSA) and the Civil Claims Agreement in Appendix B. Since a NEPA document must "fully consider the impacts of NOAA's proposed actions on the quality of the human environment" (Section 3.01 b NOAA Administrative Order Series 216-6 May 20, 1999), and "human environment" is defined in Section 6.01d of the same document to "include the relationship of people with the natural and physical environment, each EA, EIS, or SEIS must discuss interrelated

economic, social, and natural or physical environmental effects (40 CFR 1508.14)"
(emphasis added). Therefore it is essential that a detailed discussion of economic issues
which control the amount, types and effectiveness of the proposed actions as allowed or
limited by available funds be addressed.

As with any impact or effect a federal agency analyzes, NEPA requires you to take a
"hard look" at all the environmental consequences of a proposed action. See *Marsh v.
Oregon Nat '1 Resources Council*, 490 U.S. 360, 374 (1989); see also *Protect Key West,
Inc. v. Cheney*, 795 F. Supp. 1552, 1560 (S.D. Fla. 1992). This would include economic
effects or impacts.

> "identify and develop methods and procedures, in consultation with the
> Council on Environmental Quality established by title II of this Act, which
> will insure that presently unquantified environmental amenities and values
> may be given appropriate consideration in decision making along with
> economic and technical considerations ... "

NEPA Section 102 (13), 42 U.S.C. § 4332. Further, the Council on Environmental
Quality (CEQ), defines the "effects" agencies are supposed to analyze in an EA or EIS to
include economic effects or impacts.

> "Effects includes ecological (such as the effects on natural resources and
> on the components, structures, and functioning of affected ecosystems),
> aesthetic, historic, cultural, economic, social, or health, whether direct,
> indirect, or cumulative."

40 C.F.R. § 1508.8. The CEQ regulations also state that "[w]hen an environmental
impact statement is prepared and economic or social and natural or physical
environmental effects are interrelated, then the environmental impact statement will
discuss all of these effects on the human environment." 40 C.F.R. § 1508.14.

The reason I first focus on this issue is that the single most important question about
seagrass protection and restoration in the Florida Keys, besides water quality issues, is
this: will this program, as presented, significantly reduce the apparent backlog of
grounding sites needing repair (unquantified in the DPEIS), and at the same time
keep pace with the yearly increase in grounding sites and total area of damage thus
producing a NET DECREASE in the total number and area of seagrass damage
areas in the FKNMS over the next 5-10 years? In essence, is this a cost-effective plan,
or a total waste of money? Alternatives not discussed in detail include the PRIORITY
investment of all available funds, NOW, in better channel marking (emphasizing GATED
channel markers), more frequent map updates to show the channel markers, and increased
compliance monitoring, more use of boating restriction areas and enforcement of existing
laws regarding damage to submerged resources in the FKNMS. I understand that
enforcement of boating restriction areas in Pennekamp Park have been effective in

85

reducing groundings and prop scarring. The document totally ignores this good example, and these critical issues in general as priority approaches

2. Are Settlement Costs Being Estimated Accurately?

Because I am an expert witness for the U. S. Department of Justice (DOJ) on the issue of costs of restoration, I am called upon to frequently generate REAL cost estimates to do seagrass restoration after groundings in South Florida. These costs are then used to negotiate settlements of grounding cases. Money has been collected as a result. That is how I know the costs used here are 5X to 10X less than the real costs. If current settlement cases are using these low-ball estimates, the chance to really collect and expend the necessary funds to do the job right (whatever that job is) is being lost every time a settlement is reached and a check is written.

NOAA has ample evidence of their use here of a low-ball estimate. *They* have repeatedly asked experts in the field, including myself, "what are the real costs" They have asked "is there a way to reduce costs?" I and others have given them the answers. These answers are ignored in this document. My gravest concern is that the grounding numbers and size will exceed any capacity for restoration, and the conditions will get worse with time, not better. Boats are getting bigger, with bigger engines and greater draft and the operators are getting less education not more. The FKNMS has frequently publicized their efforts at seagrass education. I commend them for these awareness campaigns. However, the question about these efforts is: Are the numbers of boat groundings, size of individual boat groundings, linear miles of prop scars and the cumulative impact of all of this boat damage GOING DOWN every year as a result of these educational efforts? I know of no figures to say one way or another, but this is, again, the key issue left unanswered by this document. Can we expect, as a result of implementation of these efforts described in this DPEIS at a cost of $ _____? over_____years to achieve a significant reduction in the cumulative area of damaged seagrass in the FKNMS? I think all of the professionals who deal with this issue know, in their hearts, the answer. NOAA knows it to. It has to be addressed in this document, or we are just "rearranging the deck chairs on the Titanic."

3. Time Frames for Restoration

A third key issue I feel is left out of the discussion is a comparison of approaches to restoring grounding sites, not just methods. A general approach analysis would look at the time frames (real not made-up) between a grounding, a damage assessment, restoration, and finally return of that site to pre-impact conditions. How do we best achieve the shortest time frame for the least amount of dollars? There is not an unlimited amount of funds to get the job done, however even the real dollars available and planned to be spent are not mentioned in the document. With limited funds every other organization I deal with requires priorities and a budget that allows living within their means. Why is a budget not discussed in the document? Where is the adaptive management element of the issue of cumulative seagrass damage, rates of repair an d prevention, and dollars available to do the job in the FKNMS?

This goes to the heart of the issue of which methods to use, such as "sod replacement" I think the issue is a lot more important than addressed here. Mention is made on page 10 that "(W)here feasible, sod replacement will be done immediately after injury assessment to maximize the chance of sod survival." I agree, but what makes it "feasible" sometimes, and not "feasible" other times? Is it being done as a routine course of action on groundings in 2004?

The real focus should be on how quickly do you address restoration issues at a grounding, and what is the impact of waiting? I have mentioned above "timing" as it relates to approaches. Timing is all in grounding repair! If a triage system were applied to groundings, and an emergency response program were instituted for the larger groundings, it would mean that a team would be sent to a larger wounding site, perform an NRDA, document everything, then refill the hole using whatever materials remain from a blowout onsite, and add some more to level the site. Then the team would install at the restoration site any and all the existing plant materials randomly distributed around the site (bare-root and sods that are destined to disappear over time). Sods and bare root pieces of seagrass will regrow if properly installed (see Lewis 1987, Tomasko et al. 1991 and Lewis et al 1994 for examples).

This approach would seem to make the most sense, both ecologically and economically. Yet, in case after case that I am familiar with, the grounding takes place at time 0, an NRDA is done 4-8 months later, a restoration plan is prepared a year after that, and several years more may pass before money is collected and maybe spent on site? In the meantime, the site may repair itself, if minor, but more often, as noted by Whitfield et al (2002), and directly observed by me, with or without hurricanes, the damage gets worse as the hole is eroded, and more seagrass sods are undercut and fall away and die. Just as in human wounds, immediate action yields better results at a reduced cost. If such an approach is not a priority for consideration, then again in my professional opinion, the proposed actions would only result in the placement of a Band-Aid on a cancer.

4. Role of the Coast Guard — New Channel Markers and Informative Signage on the Water

Concerning what I perceive as the more cost-effective technique, there is an ever-so-brief mention of "water markers" in the document, and on page 54 a passing reference to coordination with the Coast Guard. I would recommend that all reference to "water markers" be changed to "aids to navigation and educational signage" to more accurately describe what is being discussed, and the issue of difficulties in permitting these essential tools to protect seagrasses be noted.

It has been my professional experience the Coast Guard ignores just about anything related to natural resources, or so they say, as their claim to fame is "navigation", not natural resource protection. I would suggest in this section that some mention be made of the real problem of the Coast Guard accepting any additional channel markers, in particular gated channel markers, as essential for safe "navigation" and protection of the nation's submerged natural resources.

It has been my professional experience that both the Florida Fish and Wildlife Conservation Commission, Division of Law Enforcement, Office of Boating and Waterways (FWC-OBW) and the Coast Guard generally oppose issuing permits for additional channel markers, in particular gated channel markers, due to the perception that this results in the placing of additional hazards in the water for some boater to run into. No matter the need to help the same boater stay off a shallow bank, and perhaps prevent injury the boater, his passengers, his boat, and most importantly the submerged resources that he grounds on. Both the FWC-OBW and the Coast Guard have to issue permits to allow installation of new or replacement channel markers, and any proposed informative signage such as a "Warning - Shallow Water Ahead" sign, and permitting is a problem if natural resource protection issues are the key reason for a permit application. I would suggest consideration of a formal MOU with the Coast Guard and the FWC-OBW, to facilitate permitting new "aids to navigation and educational signage" for safer boating and natural resource protection in the FKNMS.

5. Information Exchange and Sharing

There does not appear to be any plan for sharing information about existing actions, lessons learned, real costs, regular updates to stakeholders, etc. NOAA is preparing to spend millions of dollars on a significant issue that affects not only the FKNMS but significant other state, local and federally managed submerged resources. Other similar plans are likely in the future for Everglades and Biscayne National Parks which are contiguous with the FKNMS. What is finally decided within the context of this DPEIS process will likely be reflected in similar proposed actions at these and other sites. My personal experience to date has been that the "science" and "economics" of seagrass management and repair at the state, local and federal level is as near a black hole as the real ones. Information seems to go in, but never gets out.

As an interested stakeholder, concerned scientist and taxpayer, I sincerely request that NOAA be more forthcoming and open about NOAA seagrass management and restoration efforts, in the Keys and elsewhere. It should not be necessary for me or anyone else to file a public documents request to see what is going on, nor wait years for peer review and publication of "lessons learned." This is the age of the web. Where is the web site or sites that regularly are updated with the "Mini 312" work and other grounding restoration efforts? Are these available links adequately documented in this document? How are these to be regularly updated for interested scientists and managers?

I fully understand confidentiality in legal matters, and the desire to release only "peer reviewed and published" results. This does not stop DOJ from using my field data and professional analyses to assess damage costs and collect settlements, at which point the reports are public documents. Some level of monitoring effort and reporting related to seagrass management and restoration has been going on in the FKNMS for a long time. It is difficult for me to find any of that information. I am sure it is difficult for others too.

All professionals dealing with this complex subject would benefit from timely distribution of this important information.

I am obviously very concerned that we address these issues in order to really protect, and restore as needed, a national treasure. I am sure the answers to my questions are available and will be addressed in the next version of this document. If anyone has a question, they can call me or leave a message at 813-505-3999, 24/7.

Sincerely,

Roy R. "Robin" Lewis III, Professional Wetland Scientist, and Certified Senior Ecologist with The Ecological Society of America.

cc: Susan A. Kennedy
    Billy Causey

Literature Cited

Fonseca, M.F., W. J. Kenworthy, B.E. Julius, S. Shutter and S. Fluke. 2002. Seagrasses. Pages 149-170 in M.R. Perrow and A. J. Davy (eds.), Handbook of Ecological Restoration. Volume 2. Restoration in Practice. Cambridge University Press, Cambridge, UK.

Lewis, R.R. 1987. The restoration and creation of seagrass meadows in the southeast United States. Pages 153-173 in M.J. Durako, R.C. Phillips and R.R. Lewis, (eds.), Proceedings of the Symposium on Subtropical-Tropical Seagrasses of the Southeastern United States. Florida Marine Research Institute Pub]. 42. St. Petersburg, Florida

Lewis, R.R., C.R. Kruer, S.F. Treat and S.M. Morris. 1994. Wetland mitigation evaluation report - Florida Keys bridge replacement. State of Florida, Department of Transportation, Environmental Management Office, Tallahassee, Florida. FL-ER-5-94. 88 p + appends.

Sargent, F.J., T. J. Leary, D.W. Crewz and C.R. Kruer. 1995. Scarring of Florida's seagrasses: assessment and management options. FMRI Tech. Rep. TR-1. St. Petersburg, FL.

Tomasko, D.A., C.J. Dawes, and M.O. Hall. 1991. Effects of the number of short shoots and presence of the rhizome apical meristems on the survival and growth of transplanted seagrass, Thalassia testudinum. Contrib. Mar. Sci. 52:41-48

B.8 RESPONSE TO ROY R. "ROBIN" LEWIS, III COMMENT

I.   Magnitude of the Problem- Cumulative Area of Seagrass Impacted and the Real Costs of Restoration

I.A   Cost of Restoration

Through several calculations and reference to published material, the reviewer asserts that the DPEIS underestimates the true cost of restoration by a factor of five to ten times. This assertion is false, and the response to the declaration is as follows.

On page two of the comment, the reviewer claims that information presented in the DPEIS indicates a need for $9,438,282 to restore all seagrass injuries that have occurred as a result of vessel groundings from 1990 to 2004. The reviewer criticizes this as being off by "5X or 10X of the real costs". He implies by inclusion that the cost estimate of Fonseca *et al.* (2002) of $940,000 per hectare be used to arrive at the total of "$51,192,400 to repair and monitor all these seagrass damage sites". There are several aspects of the reviewer's comments on this matter that are erroneous.

First, the reviewer estimates that there have been 5,684 groundings over a 14-year period that resulted in seagrass damage. The reviewer then states "[u]sing the restoration cost estimate in Attachment B [of Appendix J], page 154, of $23,247,...total restoration of these 5,684 sites would require $9,438,282 to have been spent". It is unclear how the reviewer arrived at this dollar estimate. If all 5,684 seagrass groundings cost, on average, $23,247 to restore, the total restoration cost would be $132,136,000. Note that if the incorrectly calculated $9,438,282 had been off by a factor of five to ten, as suggested by the reviewer, then he would expect restoration costs to range from $47,191,000 to $94,383,000. The costs presented in Appendix J, on a per-hectare basis, are higher than those expected by the reviewer. Therefore, the reviewer's argument that NOAA is using "a low-ball estimate" (reviewer's comment, page 4) is inaccurate and without merit.

Second, the reviewer implies that the $940,000 per hectare is a more appropriate estimate. This estimate is based on a single, large grounding case that went through the litigation process. Fonseca *et al.* do not claim that this is an average of many restoration projects, nor do they claim that it is typical of seagrass restoration costs for one hectare. The reviewer's claim that the $23,247 is too low for the example scenario is not supported by his comments. The area of the example injury was 95.8 m^2. If extrapolated, this is a cost of $2,426,000 per hectare- more than the Fonseca *et al.* estimate. This invalidates the reviewer's comment that $23,247 is not enough to pay for restoration. That the per-hectare cost of the example grounding is greater than that offered by Fonseca *et al.* is not surprising. As mentioned, that was a large injury and economies of scale in restoration and monitoring were available. Such economies of scale are not available with an injury the size of the example, and a higher per-hectare cost results. Further, the $2,246,000 per hectare restoration cost extrapolated from the example injury is not directly comparable to the Fonseca *et al.* estimate for two reasons. One, the Fonseca *et al.* monitoring plan includes nine monitoring events, while the monitoring schedule shown on page 154 of the DPEIS lists only eight. If a ninth event were included in the example, the per-hectare cost would be even greater. Two, the Fonseca *et al.* estimate includes federal assessment costs and interest. The $23,247 listed for the example case is clearly labeled "subtotal" on page 154 and does not include an assessment costs or interest. Again, including these costs in the example extrapolation would further expand the difference between the two estimates.

Third, the reviewer "assumes that each [grounding that occurred in seagrass meadows] is approximately the size of the example given". He uses this assumption to support the use of $23,247 as a typical restoration cost per grounding. This assumption is invalid. The vast majority of vessel groundings in seagrass meadows do not result in the magnitude of injury described by the example grounding. However, the example is fairly typical of the small subset of seagrass groundings that will have natural resource damage assessments completed and restoration undertaken.

Since the draft regional restoration plan was written, NOAA has revised the cost estimate assumptions. The cost estimates for the example have been updated for the FPEIS. The restoration, monitoring, and oversight costs for the example are currently estimated to total $24,408, and increase of $1,161. The responses to the reviewer's comments provided in this section are still valid in light of this change.

I.B   Adequacy of the Restoration Program

On page two of the comment, the reviewer poses numerous questions that he claims the PEIS should address. The questions can be summarized as being related to two topics: the cost of restoration and the amount of restoration that has been completed. The first topic was addressed above. The second topic is largely irrelevant. As noted in the "Purpose" section of the DPEIS on page one, the "document focuses on **future** regional seagrass restoration and injury prevention activities" (emphasis added). Restoration efforts to date are not within the scope of the DPEIS, with the exception of how lessons learned are incorporated in the evaluation of each of the restoration options.

Further, the reviewer claims on comment page two that the injuries documented by Sargent *et al.* (1995) "appears not to be documented nor discussed as a problem needing to be addressed in the document". Contrary to this claim, the Sargent *et al.* data is referenced in the Regional Restoration Plan (Appendix J, page 139). Orphan seagrass injuries, such as those detailed by Sargent *et al.*, will be addressed as compensatory restoration projects for NRDA cases. Thus, the DPEIS not only identifies a source of funding[8] for restoring orphan injuries, it outlines how such restorations will be selected and prioritized.

I.C   Examination of the Economic Effects of Proposed Actions

The reviewer provides several citations that require, among other things, that the economic effects of proposed activities be analyzed. The reviewer does not appear to differentiate between potential economic effects of undertaking seagrass restoration and the financial cost that must be incurred to complete that restoration. The criteria for examining the socioeconomic effects of potential actions are detailed on pages 25 and 26 of the DPEIS. The regional economic activity and demographic changes in the region of influence are discussed for the ten restoration options in chapter four.

II.   Are Settlement Costs Being Estimated Accurately?

II.A   Cost of Restoration

The reviewer again raises the issue of restoration costs, and claims that, "the costs used here are 5X to 10X less than the real costs". This duplicative comment was responded to above. Further, the purpose of the DPEIS is to evaluate "the short and long-term environmental and socioeconomic effects related to the implementation of seagrass restoration and seagrass injury prevention projects" (page 1). A discussion of the cost of individual restoration projects is beyond the scope of this programmatic document.

II.B   The Effect of Seagrass Educational Campaigns

The reviewer requests information on the success of past educational efforts in the FKNMS. It is widely recognized that quantifying the benefits of any educational or outreach program, regardless of subject, is exceedingly difficult. Given the multitude of factors, a causal relationship between a change in societal behavior and public education/outreach can rarely be definitively established. Additionally, the studies that must be undertaken to attempt this quantification would likely cost more than the education/outreach campaigns they are designed to measure. For these reasons, the FKNMS has not attempted to answer the question, "[a]re the number of boat

---

[8] The "Purpose" of the DPEIS states "the types of seagrass restoration and injury prevention projects…will be implemented with funds collected through natural resource damage assessment (NRDA) settlements" (page 1).

groundings, size of individual boat groundings, linear miles of prop scars and the cumulative impact of all of this boat damage GOING DOWN every year as a result of these educational efforts?".

II.C   Sufficiency of the Program

The author questions whether the program described in the DPEIS will be sufficient to reverse the claim of deteriorating condition of seagrass communities in the Florida Keys. First, data suggest that seagrass communities in the FKNMS are stable and have been for several years (Peterson and Fourqurean 2001). Claims that overall condition of seagrass is declining are not supported by published reports. Second, numerous authors agree that the largest threats to seagrass communities in south Florida are declining water quality and increasing coastal development. Inducing an improvement in the stable state of seagrasses in the FKNMS would require significant effort to ameliorate these two threats. It is beyond the scope of this program to address either water quality or coastal development issues. The purpose of the restoration program described in the DPEIS is to repair the most harmful seagrass injuries caused by small vessel groundings. The document makes no representations as to the program's ability to effect overall seagrass community health in the FKNMS.

III.   Time Frames for Restoration

III.A   Budget

The reviewer criticizes the DPEIS for omitting a discussion of the budget to be associated with the seagrass restoration activities described in the document. Specifically, the reviewer states "[t]he real dollars available and planned to be spent are not mentioned in the document", and asks "[w]hy is a budget not discussed in the document?". As mentioned above, the "Purpose" of the DPEIS declares that the funds to implement and monitor the restoration activities described in the document will come from natural resource damage assessment settlements. Thus, there is no budget for restoration activities to discuss.

III.B   Sod Replacement

The reviewer comments that the discussion of sod replacement as a restoration technique is not given proper weight in comparison to other techniques. Specifically, the reviewer asks what makes sod replacement " 'feasible' sometimes, and not 'feasible' other times?" and asks if it is a routine course of action. The text describing sod replacement on page 10 was clarified in the FPEIS. There are two primary considerations with the use of the sod replacement option. First, if there are no large chunks of dislodged seagrass with intact rhizomes, then replacement is not feasible (it is impossible). Most groundings do not produce large, dislodged chunks. It is much more common for the vessel to grind the seagrass into small pieces. Second, if the blowhole or scar/trench requires sediment fill to bring it back to grade, then sod replacement is not feasible. The act of filling the injury after settlement would simply kill the replaced sod. However, this technique is always used in those relatively rare groundings that produce intact sod chunks and do not require sediment fill.

III.C   Triage System

The reviewer notes that it would be more beneficial to triage all seagrass injuries from vessel groundings shortly after they occur. We agree with the reviewer's comment. However, as funds to implement restoration are derived from natural resource damage assessment settlements, NOAA currently does not have the financial ability to enact emergency restoration at all vessel grounding sites prior to settlement. NOAA is currently exploring sources of funding to conduct emergency restoration.

IV.   Role of the Coast Guard – New Channel Markers and Informative Signage on the Water

IV.A   Aids to Navigation and Educational Signage

The reviewer recommends that the term "water markers" be changed to "aids to navigation and educational signage". The term was altered in the FPEIS to clarify its meaning.

IV.B   MOU with the Coast Guard

The reviewer properly notes that both the Coast Guard and the Florida Fish and Wildlife Conservation Commission issue permits for the installation of channel markers. The reviewer claims that both agencies "generally oppose issuing permits for additional channel markers, in particular gated channel markers, due to the perception that this results in the placing of additional hazards in the water". The reviewer suggests that NOAA enter into a formal MOU with these two agencies to facilitate permitting of new channel markers. We do not believe that a formal MOU is necessary to facilitate the permitting process. Installation of channel markers is considered on a case-by-case basis. If data suggests that additional markers in a certain area would decrease boating accidents, then NOAA would support the installation of markers at that location. However, such suggestive data is lacking. In addition, a significant number of the reported groundings occur in the vicinity of existing water markers. This suggests that improved boater education, not additional markers, may be more effective at decreasing vessel grounding frequency.

V.   Information Exchange and Sharing

The reviewer requests "NOAA be more forthcoming and open about NOAA seagrass management and restoration efforts". In addition, the reviewer inquires about a website to describe the restoration program and its results. We believe this point is beyond the scope of the DPEIS. However, there are ongoing plans for the development of a website devoted to seagrass and coral restoration in the Florida Keys. This project will progress as staffing and budget permit.